Praise for *The Vision Code*

'Most people think vision is something you are born with. Either you have it or you don't. But from reading Oleg Konovalov's *The Vision Code*, you will learn that vision is a competence that you can nurture – by thinking boldly, keeping an open mind and getting out of your own way. As a CEO, I've come to realize from reading *The Vision Code* that vision is my single most valuable tool. It literally allows you to choose your company's future'.

The Vision Code is a fascinating blueprint for mastering a vision and becoming a true visionary'.

Eric Schurenberg, CEO at *Inc.* and *Fast Company*

'Vision is essential to successful leadership, but often misunderstood and poorly conceived. In this insightful guide, Oleg Konovalov lays out his own compelling vision for what visionary leadership consists of and where its value lies, presenting it as a simple yet very practical business tool. *The Vision Code* defines a new stage in visionary leadership development'.

Courtney Fingar, editor-in-chief, *FDI*, New Statesman Media Group

'Success thrives on a clear and vivid vision that is a property of a few so far. Being able to craft an inspiring vision is what makes the difference between great leaders and conventional managers. So far, it has been thought that visionary leaders are born, that it is a natural gift for solely a few lucky ones. Yet, Oleg's book, *The Vision Code*, proves the contrary. In a very engaging way, Oleg's book walks us through a series of interviews and teaches us that every manager can learn how to draft a compelling and inspiring vision.

Having a vision of a vision is a superior mastery that Oleg Konovalov used for presenting vision as a practical business tool accessible to all. *The Vision Code* changes the rules of the game in today's fast-changing world'.

Antonio Nieto-Rodriguez, a World Champion in Project Management, Thinkers50 'Ideas into Practice' Award, PMI Past Chair, co-founder of the Strategy Implementation Institute and the global movement Brightline

'*The Vision Code* is a remarkable book. Thanks to Oleg Konovalov, vision is no longer a fuzzy concept. It is a powerful management tool that thrives on courage but also on relevance. Vision has value only if it is implementable and has an impact. *The Vision Code* explores how it is achieved. In doing so, Oleg Konovalov has contributed significantly to establishing the theory of vision on firm ground. You should read this book not once, but twice!'

Stephane Garelli, founder of World Competitiveness Center, ex-Managing Director at the World Economic Forum, Professor Emeritus at IMD business school and the University of Lausanne, Switzerland

'A crucial element for leadership success, vision is often tough to develop. Read *The Vision Code* for an in-depth exploration of what it is and how to achieve it!'

Sanyin Siang, Thinkers50 #1 Leadership Coach & Mentor

'*The Vision Code* demystifies the process of defining and following through on a vision, which will become increasingly important as the pace of change accelerates. The compelling stories and examples from leaders across industries and geographies underscore the importance of vision as ideal as well as practical tools to achieving it'.

Deepa Prahalad, design strategist, co-author *Predictable Magic*, Thinkers50 India

'When you have a vision, work becomes an adventure! This beautiful book will inspire the best in you to create your own vision and your own adventure. It is all here for you to discover. Don't miss the chance for a more meaningful career and life! Read, study and share this treasure!'

Chester Elton, the 'Apostle of Appreciation', bestselling author of *The Carrot Principle*, *All In*, and *Leading with Gratitude*

'In this critical, must-read book, Dr. Oleg Konovalov demystifies the practice of creating and achieving a vision, in both professional and personal contexts. His guidance is clear and pragmatic, bringing to light the knowledge that, without strong vision, our purpose cannot be fulfilled. In his search for the golden ratio of vision, he surfaced an exceptionally practical six-step model on how to create and execute vision. He is the visionary of visionaries and can help us all with our life and business destiny'.

Jennifer McCollum, CEO, Linkage, Inc.

'Oleg Konovalov is the "Whisperer of Vision". He opens a new page in understanding vision and how to make it a reality. *The Vision Code* is an incredible contribution to the business world and to visionary leadership in particular, making it accessible to millions of modern leaders'.

Benjamin Croft, founder and Chairman, WBECS Group

'*The Vision Code* provides a compelling framework, clear narrative and a sound framework to decode what is a real vision in organisations. Yet, the book is not only deep and fascinating but also extremely practical by providing a roadmap, examples, storytelling. Is a truly remarkable book we cannot afford to miss'.

Paolo Gallo, bestselling author of *The Compass & The Radar*, ex-Chief Human Resources Officer at the World Economic Forum

'Oleg Konovalov is the true whisperer of vision who reveals its practical nature. In his *The Vision Code*, he offers a simple six-step business tool for creating, constructing, and executing a strong vision. The ultimate reading for all modern leaders'.

Charlene Li, founder of Altimeter, a Prophet Company, *New York Times* bestselling author of *The Disruption Mindset*

'*The Vision Code* is packed full of insights and great examples of the value of a clear, compelling vision. Of particular value is the section on execution – an often-neglected aspect of developing a vision: You have to make it real. The book presents a rich, multidimensional view of organizational and personal vision that will expand and enhance any leader's perspective'.

David B. Peterson, PhD, Senior Director, Executive Coaching & Development, Google LLC

'Vision is a topic that we all think we know, so much so that we ignore it. Dr. Oleg Konovalov does not. His new book, *The Vision Code*, is an exploration into the origins of vision and its importance to our personal and business lives. Through his comprehensive research and real-life practice, Dr. Oleg Konovalov demystifies vision and presents it as a very practical business tool. *The Vision Code* is a must-read for those leaders seeking to define the future in ways that allow organisations, teams and individuals to succeed'.

John Baldoni, Global Gurus Top 30, Inc.com Top 50 Leadership Expert, bestselling author of 14 books published in 10 languages

'Having a detailed and compelling vision for a vision is a property of wizards capable of changing the world and helping others become visionaries. In his groundbreaking book, *The Vision Code*, Dr. Oleg Konovalov offers an ultimate and powerful practical toolkit for visionary leaders of all levels. I encourage you to read this book. *The Vision Code* is one of the most important books that can change your life and business'.

Mohammed Naser Hamdan Al Zaabi,
Director of the Trade Promotion Department, UAE Ministry of Economy

'Oleg Konovalov is the "Wizard of Vision". With *The Vision Code*, he takes the fuzzy concept of vision and turns it into a practical, versatile and essential tool that helps leaders position themselves as visionaries. I highly recommend this book. It's rich with wisdom and full of lessons we can put to immediate use'.

Sally Helgesen, bestselling author of *How Women Rise*,
The Female Vision and *The Web of Inclusion*

'I love Oleg Konovalov's book and it's messages and teachings around vision. Establishing a strong vision is the single most important step for embarking on a change process. All executives and leaders should read Oleg's book because it breaks down the elements and practices of visionary leadership. Visionary leaders manage their energy rather than time – which is such an important concept for everyone to understand and perhaps most importantly to respect. Everyone should strive to be a visionary leader, which will help them become aligned with their own individual goals and corporate goals, become more driven toward positive outcomes and focus core values and purpose in life. Bravo Oleg! Awesome work!'

Louis Carter, CEO of Best Practice Institute and
author of 11 leadership and management books including
Change Champions Field Guide and *In Great Company*

'*The Vision Code* is a masterpiece that makes you rethink the way you live and do business. The new perspectives that this book presents to you are truly unique and enlightening, and in a league of their own. It will help you find and execute your very own strong vision through the simple six-step process. I found myself wanting to change and rethink my company's vision and at the same time start working on my own personal life vision'.
Oleg Konovalov's *The Vision Code* is a fantastic and powerful book. Do yourself a favour and read it!'

Rene Viborg, founder and CEO, Zylinc

'In *The Vision Code*, Oleg Konovalov brilliantly demystifies vision and cracks the code for us by revealing the inner and outer anatomy of visionary leadership. This book is a must-read for leaders who see what others cannot see yet and want to lead their people on a journey of successful execution'.

Nicole Heimann, CEO, Nicole Heimann & Partners AG, author of *How to Develop the Authentic Leader in You*, Marshall Goldsmith Thinkers 50 'Leading Global Coach' Award

'In *The Vision Code*, Oleg Konovalov masterfully shares how the best leaders and highest performing companies have clear and compelling visions that guide them personally as well as their organisations. He brings the concept of vision from the abstract to the tangible and actionable and shares the keys to developing a vision that is both grounded and serves as a compelling North Star'.

Robert Glazer, WSJ bestselling author of *Elevate*, *Friday Forward* and *Performance Partnerships*

'If you think you have vision and clarity of purpose in your business, this book will shatter that notion. Dr. Oleg Konovalov, in his new book, *The Vision Code*, will change the way you see things as a leader. Dr. Konovalov helps us break the secret code to a positive and prosperous future by showing us how to create a strong vision that inspires and how to execute on that vision as a leader. This book is an absolute must-read!'

Rhett Power, *Forbes* columnist, co-founder at Courageous Leadership

'In these unprecedented times, having a clear and strong vision is more important than ever before. We have a chance to recalibrate the way we live and work and make this world a better place. Envisioning the future we want to create is an important part of this process. This book provides a unique and practical approach to developing and implementing a vision and turning it into reality. I warmly welcome this long-anticipated book'.

Prof. Vlatka Hlupic, one of the most influential HR thinkers, author of The *Management Shift* and *Humane Capital*

'It is rare in the business expert arena when one expert corners the market on a specific topic. With this book, Dr. Konovalov has cornered the market on "vision". His dissection of "vision," it's elements and the process of creating a vision is nothing short of genius. Bravo for providing a road map for all to follow'.

Dr. Terry Jackson, thought leader, MG100 Coach, author of
Transformational Thinking

'In *The Vision Code*, Dr. Oleg Konovalov masterfully guides us into creating our vision. This book is informative, authentic and inspirational. It is a must-read. I encourage all to read it and learn from it'.

Dr. Abraham Khoureis, PhD, author and host of *Leadership &
Politics Show with Dr. Abraham*

The Vision
Code

The Vision Code

How to Create and Execute a Compelling Vision for Your Business

Oleg Konovalov

WILEY

This edition first published 2021

© 2021 by Oleg Konovalov

Registered office

John Wiley & Sons Ltd, The Atrium, Southern Gate, Chichester, West Sussex, PO19 8SQ, United Kingdom

For details of our global editorial offices, for customer services and for information about how to apply for permission to reuse the copyright material in this book please see our website at www.wiley.com.

Wiley publishes in a variety of print and electronic formats and by print-on-demand. Some material included with standard print versions of this book may not be included in e-books or in print-on-demand. If this book refers to media such as a CD or DVD that is not included in the version you purchased, you may download this material at http://booksupport.wiley.com. For more information about Wiley products, visit www.wiley.com.

Designations used by companies to distinguish their products are often claimed as trademarks. All brand names and product names used in this book are trade names, service marks, trademarks or registered trademarks of their respective owners. The publisher is not associated with any product or vendor mentioned in this book.

Limit of Liability/Disclaimer of Warranty: While the publisher and author have used their best efforts in preparing this book, they make no representations or warranties with respect to the accuracy or completeness of the contents of this book and specifically disclaim any implied warranties of merchantability or fitness for a particular purpose. It is sold on the understanding that the publisher is not engaged in rendering professional services and neither the publisher nor the author shall be liable for damages arising herefrom. If professional advice or other expert assistance is required, the services of a competent professional should be sought.

Library of Congress Cataloging-in-Publication Data is available:

ISBN 9781119775911 (hardback)
ISBN 9781119775935 (ePDF)
ISBN 9781119775928 (ePub)

Cover Design: Wiley
Cover Image: © GeorgePeters/Getty Images

Set in 12/15pt JansonTextLTStd by SPi Global, Chennai, India
Printed and bound by CPI Group (UK) Ltd, Croydon, CR0 4YY

10 9 8 7 6 5 4 3 2 1

Contents

Foreword

Over the past four decades, I have made a living coaching and educating leaders globally. In doing so, I've come to be the #1 Leadership thinker and #1 Executive Coach in the world. I do this because I have a purpose. I help others become what and who they can be. I help successful people become more successful, and this requires a convincing vision that will resonate with people.

Life does not matter without a purpose. Are you making progress, are you achieving something, are you happy, are you in a good relationship, are you doing what you love doing?

In the world of business, people tend to think that purpose is about money. Here's the dirty secret, money doesn't matter that much. It is a by-product of what you do, a tool to allow you to do more. The truth is, if you have enough money for a moderate lifestyle, money does not matter much. Once basic needs are fulfilled, money is superfluous.

So, what is purpose then? What is it that will reveal meaning in your life? In purely practical terms, it is helping others in some way. And to help others, you need a vision on how to do that.

If you have no vision, why are you here? If all you are doing is eating, breathing and going about daily tasks, you already know that is a life devoid of purpose.

You picked up this book because you know you are missing something. You are missing the thing that will make your life and business meaningful.

This feeling is shared by many, perhaps especially by leaders. Modern leadership depends on vision and direction. If we are getting better with a direction, many still struggle with vision, thinking it unnecessary or that it is beyond them.

Top global thought leader Oleg Konovalov has an incredible sense of exploring new areas in leadership and management. With this book, *The Vision Code*, Oleg has proven himself as the da Vinci of visionary leadership.

The Vision Code is a breakthrough book that sets the foundations for a new school of thought. It re-evaluates and reimagines the world of corporations, not to mention our personal lives as lived purposefully. This book puts vision into the spotlight, elevating it beyond a mere mission statement to its rightful place as a fundamental part of long-term success.

With Oleg's guidance, we can understand and break the code to create and structure a clear and compelling vision, how to communicate it and lead it, and above all how to live by it with integrity.

This book presents the creation and development of vision in a simple six-step process, making it accessible to those thinking momentary and the practical, beyond the bottom line. It is a practical guide for leaders of all sorts, as well as a very effective tool for visionary leadership coaching.

Oleg Konovalov does not merely rely on his sole store of experience and wisdom. He has spent months interviewing other visionary leaders from around the world and shares their insights throughout *The Vision Code*. The vision is no longer a mystery. It has been elegantly decoded by the master of visionary leadership.

The flow of the book has been carefully designed to take the reader on the vision journey leading to the final destination: from why you need a vision, to how implement it, to re-evaluating the whole process along the way.

As I read *The Vision Code*, I frequently asked myself: 'What can I do better?' Such a simple question – and yet, a question that, when you actively think about it, transforms your life. If you ask 'What can be done better in this book?' the answer is – 'Nothing!' This book decodes vision and presents the practical tools and sophisticated knowledge needed for leaders to put it at the forefront of their businesses to make a positive, lasting difference.

This book will reinvent you and others around you. Your journey to your successful future starts here.

Life is good.

—Marshall Goldsmith
Only two-time Thinkers 50 #1 Leadership
Thinker in the world
#1 Executive Coach

INTRODUCTION
In Search of the Golden Ratio of Vision

We are living in a time of leadership blindness. All leaders claim to have a vision. At best, the vast majority are only pretending. In truth, about 0.1% of business, social or political leaders actually have a vision.

Modern leaders often cannot explain what vision is and how it can be made a reality. They substitute money and performance indicators for vision, forgetting that, without vision, no amount of time, money or resources can help. As Carl Jung suggested, 'Until you make the unconscious conscious, it will direct your life and you will call it fate'.

The reality of the Digital Age revealed that, while we mention the importance of vision daily, the majority of people have little if any understanding of it. Yet, a solid vision is a necessary foundation for any successful organisation.

We desperately need leaders of all levels to be armed with an understanding of vision as never before. Without this, there will be no long-term progress.

We desperately need more visionary leaders. Visionaries such as Lee Kuan Yew (16 September 1923 to 23 March 2015), the first Prime Minister of Singapore, transformed the country from a 'third world country to a first world country in a single generation'; Carl Gustav Mannerheim (4 June 1867 to 27 January 1951), the President of Finland, is still voted as the greatest Finn of all time and the father of modern Finland; and Nelson Mandela (18 July 1918 to 5 December 2013), a South African anti-apartheid revolutionary, political leader and philanthropist who served as President of South Africa from 1994 to 1999, is named 'the father of the nation' and 'a global icon'. There are many others to whom we still pay tribute.

Vision as We See It

What we do really understand about vision?

Having a vision and being able to a make it a reality differentiates leaders from managers. When there is no vision, no amount of effort or money can help. With vision, real change can be achieved. The world is conquered by visionaries and surrenders its advantages and opportunities to them unconditionally. Even the most sophisticated and time-tested system can be defeated by someone with a sufficiently strong vision.

Vision creates the fertile ground on which we build the future. How we create a productive and prosperous space – for all stakeholders, employees, customers, partners and future users of this eco-system – depends on visionary leaders.

Having a vision is like looking at the present from the future's standpoint. Being a visionary is similar to putting one's own signature on the future while being here and now. A visionary defines how soon the future reality will come. In this sense, vision is like a time machine. In looking from a desired future back to the present, one can envision all the steps needed to get from here to there.

There is only a slim chance for success, breakthrough initiatives, incredible achievements and an abundance of opportunities in a flat, two-dimensional reality. A solid vision opens up a multidimensional space in which anything is possible. Vision is the most powerful and versatile tool we have to make a difference in the world around us.

Questioning the Understanding of Vision

The future will come whether you have a vision or not. But without a vision, you will be lost. It will be a reality you don't accept as it doesn't reflect your desires. And if you don't have a vision, do any desires you have even matter?

I've been thinking about this for the past 24 years. I even remember the start of this path as if it happened yesterday. I climbed to the top of a mountain in the middle of nowhere. I sat at the top and gazed around into this great tranquil wilderness, basking in the solitude.

Suddenly I realised how little, powerless, inconsequential, imperceptible and insignificant I am compared with this world. Something whispered within me – 'what is the meaning of what I do? What do I do for the future? Who am I, and where do I want to be? How I can escape mediocrity?' Since then I've been thinking about vision from different angles.

A vision cannot be bought. It can't be merely found. It has to be created.

In this book, we will thoroughly explore the concept of vision. Why is it important, and for whom? How do visionaries define vision, and how do they experience it? What common leadership and personal traits are shared by visionaries? What is the difference between ordinary and visionary leadership? If we consider vision as a mental or psychological construction, then what elements of it are the most critical? How do these incredible leaders construct their vision and make it a reality? How do visionaries prepare or reinvent themselves to make a vision a reality? How do they act as visionaries and constructors of a positive future? What struggles and difficulties do they face, and how do they overcome them?

In searching for answers and practical solutions, I decided to talk with today's visionaries, those who are changing the way people work and live, to open a window into how they think, act and construct their vision.

I decided to discuss these questions with 19 exceptional visionaries from across the globe, representing different industries and backgrounds:

- Marshall Goldsmith, #1 Leadership Thinker in the world
- Martin Lindstrom, #1 Branding expert in the world
- Garry Ridge, Chairman and CEO of WD-40 Company
- David Katz, founder and CEO of Plastic Bank
- Stuart Crainer, co-founder, Thinkers50
- John Spence, one of the top 100 business thought leaders in the world and business advisor to companies worldwide
- Feyzi Fatehi, CEO of Corent Tech, Inc.
- Olga Uskova, President and founder of Cognitive Technologies Group
- Mark Thompson, world's #1 CEO Coach, 30 Global Gurus and a Venture Investor
- Asheesh Advani, President and CEO of Junior Achievement (JA) Worldwide
- Adam Witty, founder and CEO of Advantage Media/ ForbesBooks
- H.E. Ms. Sania A. Ansari, Chairperson at Ansari Group Ltd and Chairperson at United Refugee Green Council Canada
- Thomas Kolditz, PhD, Executive Director, Doerr Institute for New Leaders at Rice University, Brigadier General (Retired)
- Prof. Amit Kapoor, Chairman of Institute for Competitiveness, India
- Alex Goryachev, Managing Director at Cisco Innovation Centers, *Wall Street Journal* bestselling author of *Fearless Innovation*

- Noel Ferguson, founder and Executive Chairman of Institute of One World Leadership (IOWL)
- Prof. Nabhit Kapur, Psy.D, founder of PeacefulMind Foundation
- Raphael Louis, Leader and President of the National Coalition Party of Canada (NCPC)
- Dr. Babalola Omoniyi, founder and Executive Director of Pan African Leadership and Entrepreneurship Development Centre (PALEDEC)

These people are simply exceptional, and I will introduce them and their stories in the pages of this book. They enthusiastically shared their personal stories, painstaking experience, invaluable lessons and practical recommendations.

In Search of the Golden Ratio

It might seem like it is enough to find the answers to these questions by gleaning the best that these visionaries have to offer and synthesising them in to a whole. Still, my pragmatic entrepreneurial mind said – *no, what else can I offer?*

Vision holds the secret code to a positive and prosperous future. But how can we break this code?

The *golden ratio* or the *divine proportion* as a term was coined by Luca Pacioli in his book *De Divina Proportione* (*The Divine Proportion*), published in 1509. This book was illustrated by Leonardo Da Vinci with three-dimensional geometric solids and templates for script letters in calligraphy, and this is why the idea of the golden ratio is often attributed to him. Da Vinci's masterpieces *The Last Supper*, *La Jaconde* (*Mona Lisa*) and *The Vitruvian Man* made use of the golden ratio.

The golden ratio describes the beauty sensed in the harmony and proportion in different spheres such as art, nature, math, design and the human body. We subconsciously prefer and admire objects and shapes that properly use the golden ratio.

Luca Pacioli defined his approach as 'a work necessary for all clear-sighted and inquiring human minds, in which everyone who loves to study philosophy, perspective, painting, sculpture, architecture, music and other mathematical disciplines will find a very delicate, subtle and admirable teaching and will delight in diverse questions touching on a very secret science' (Meisner, G.B. 2018).

This book attempts to find the golden ratio of vision and unlock this secret knowledge.

How to Read This Book

Using the analogy of the butterfly effect that describes how small things can have a dramatic impact on complex systems, we can look at vision as a beautiful butterfly that causes enormous changes in the world. It is born somewhere inside of a visionary's mind and soul, and the visionary decides to give it wings of a certain shape and colour. Then this beauty learns how to spread those wings and fly, creating a new reality and changing the world. As Neil Gaiman and Terry Pratchett wrote in *Good Omens* (2011), 'a butterfly flaps its wings in the Amazonian jungle, and subsequently a storm ravages half of Europe'.

I structured the discussion of vision using the same principle as it reflects the four natural stages of a vision's development. *Part One: Creation* discusses why vision is important, how it comes about and what is needed to create it. *Part Two: Making Vision Strong* sheds light on the core criteria, elements and characteristics of a vivid vision and highlights how leaders should prepare themselves for reaching new heights. *Part Three: Execution* dives into how to make vision a reality and turn it into a practical business tool. *Part Four: Visionary You* looks into how visionaries think and offers recommendations for everyday use.

Let's Break Ground

We are brought into this world as creators, and whether we fulfil our purpose or not entirely depends on our ability to craft a vision and inspire others to share in it. Vision is the core property of those who are shaping the future today, and we can't ignore it without ignoring future prospects – whether business or personal.

I invite you to join me on this journey in search of the golden ratio of vision, regardless of whether you are a mature leader or someone at the first stages of your growth. The reward will be not just a well-crafted vision, but the ability to lead others in making that vision a reality.

Part I

Creation

1

Making the Unconscious Conscious, or Why Vision Is Important

'Leadership is lifting of a man's vision to higher sights'.

Peter Drucker

Vision is a meaningless term. . . unless we truly understand its importance and value. If people don't fully understand the importance of vision for themselves and others, they will never appreciate someone else's vision, its greatness and prominence.

Someone who has never been exposed to classical music will not appreciate a symphony. For him or her, Beethoven's *Moonlight Sonata* isn't something beautiful but annoying and even depressing.

Personally, it would be difficult to build a strong happy family without a vision created around love, respect, care and mutual support. Otherwise, it is a mere social change with little chance for real happiness.

The same situation can be found in different businesses, social projects and political movements regardless of their size, industry or country. People just nod their heads and pay lip service to a vision without really buying it, regarding it as meaningless talk.

We are in a strange situation where vision is praised or even idolised but often not sufficiently appreciated. Glass half empty or glass half full is only a matter of enthusiasm. What is poured into the glass is what matters most.

What meaning we assign to a given vision defines its importance for personal life and business. Revealing the nature of something previously considered impossible allows us to make it understandable for many, which allows them to participate in the vision's further development. Let's look at why vision is important and how successful leaders use it.

There are at least seven core factors of a vision's importance for business and personal life. Vision provides purpose and defines the future; it gives an answer to that critical 'why', allowing us to break out of a negative reality, and unites people by providing a source of inspiration for how we live our lives.

Defining Purpose

We spend much of our lives justifying our worthiness for having it, how we fulfil the opportunities offered and obligations placed on us and what kind of success stories we can write that are worth sharing. Judging a life's worthiness can truly be done only at the end, after the life is lived. Vision helps craft a plan on how to live that good life.

Vision is a core around which all those stories are written. If it's there then we have something to write and share. If not, life becomes a collection of loose ends, leaving one feeling lost and unfulfilled.

How does vision reflect purpose? How far can we go in life and business without vision? For whom is vision important? I addressed these questions to Marshall Goldsmith:

Marshall Goldsmith is the only two-time Thinkers 50 #1 Leadership Thinker in the world. He has been recognised by Thinkers50, Fast Company, *INC* magazine and Global Gurus as the World's Leading Executive Coach. Marshall is a top authority on leadership and executive coaching. He is, in fact, the inventor of leadership coaching and today helps successful leaders become even more successful. His Pay-it-Forward initiative turned into the Marshall Goldsmith 100 Coaches global program that helps thousands of leaders achieve new levels of success.

Marshall has written three *New York Times* and *Wall Street Journal* bestsellers – *Triggers*, *MOJO* and *What Got You Here Won't Get You There*. The editors of Amazon.com have recognised *Triggers* and *What Got You Here Won't Get You There* as being in the Top 100 leadership and success books ever written.

'*Look at life itself first. What matters most is having a purpose. Are you making progress, are you achieving something, are you happy, do you have great relationships, and do you engage with what you are doing? Why are we here? To me our vision should be reflective of our purpose. Our vision makes our purpose come to life.*

I can think of differentiating two levels, micro level and macro level. At the micro level, vision is important for everyone because if you have no vision for your life, then you have no real purpose. You have no real goal. You're just drifting through life.

At the macro level, it is important for any organization to have a vision. Where are we going collectively? Because without this collective vision, how can the individual know how they can contribute to the future of the organization?

If you are a knowledge worker, this is important. If knowledge workers know more about what they're doing, then it is important that their leader has a strong vision so he can continue to lead them.

If you are a factory worker in an assembly line, then this is a reasonably meaningless concept. The company may or may not have a vision but as far as your life goes, it's pretty irrelevant as you're doing the same thing every day.

If you look at our history, we can see how the world and certain traits evolved. Before, an entire system was designed to promote the superiority of the upper class, the master was always better than the apprentice. The apprentice was there to learn from the master. The master was superior. Even if you look at pretty much the entire history of leadership, the leader was always superior to the people being led. It's no longer true. This is the big change today. Leaders are not inherently superior to the people they are leading. You're leading people who have superior knowledge to you, which is a whole new world. You can't tell them what to do and how to do it. Imagine a situation where I communicate no vision to you, but you are just there to do what you are told. Why bother to communicate a vision because you're just there to move things from here to there? On the other hand, if you're a knowledge worker, the opposite is true. If we don't have a larger vision, how can my knowledge worker colleague figure out how to help us achieve a vision if you don't know what it is? You have to have this much more macro level knowledge in order to make a positive difference for the organizations today'.

A journey cannot be completed or even correctly planned without vision. As David Viscott said in his book *Finding Your Strength in Difficult Times: A Book of Meditations* (1993), 'The purpose of life is to discover your gift. The work of life is to develop it. The meaning of life is to give your gift away'.

A recipe for an unhappy life is to agree with everything and persuade yourself that nothing needs improvement. This is a sure way to get disconnected and lose oneself for nothing. Being happy and enjoying life requires vision. Thus, by following a vision we can fulfil the micro level – live a happy and satisfying personal life.

To fulfil the macro level, we need to live for others as all great leaders do. Today, vision is even more important as we witness a time of redefinition of leadership and the role of leaders, from being superiors to leader-servants. A leader-servant is one who uses vision to serve people beyond their own interests. At this level, vision is needed to define and communicate how to help many people make their lives fulfilling and meaningful.

Answering 'Why'

The times of hunting to survive are long gone. We evolved as humans to a much higher level by asking a simple question – why? In this sense, the highest form of questioning is asking the 'why' about oneself and the purpose of existence. This three-letter word has the ultimate power over the way we see ourselves and the world around us. 'Why' is a question caused by our curiosity as to how we can do something better and finding a compelling reasoning for changing ourselves.

Vision points to the most fulfilling answer to that personal 'why'. I discussed this point with Garry Ridge, who is excellent at moving boundaries and finding answers to difficult problems by asking 'why?' Garry Ridge is the Chairman and CEO of WD-40 Company, which is a San Diego, California-based manufacturer of household and multi-use products, including its signature brand, WD-40, which is sold in 176 countries. You probably have one of those WD-40 cans in your garage or under a kitchen sink. Don't forget that all Formula-1 and other racing car teams use WD-40 for solving problems on a daily basis as well in the middle of a race. The company's success is crystallised in the company's vision statement 'The success of the WD-40 Company is people just like you, whether you're a tribe member, business partner, investor or customer'.

'I think people today are searching for purpose. I think that a clearly defined vision is not really just a vision but it's an answer to why we exist. If you have a clearly defined purpose or a vision people can then be involved in what you do because it's meaningful to them.

We often say – imagine a place where you go to work every day and you make a contribution to something bigger than yourself. I think a vision is a description of something that's bigger than ourselves.

I have a vision for my life or a 'why' statement where I have the most wonderful job in the world. I wake up every day to help people create positive lasting memories where the most exciting part of that is finding all the different ways to do it. So that's my vision, that's my purpose. It does stay in line with the vision or the purpose of the WD-40 Company. The company exists to create positive lasting memories by solving problems in factories, homes, and workshops around the world. We solve problems and we create opportunities. I'm fortunate that I've been able to get comfortable aligning my personal vision or my personal 'why' and the WD-40 vision and align them very closely'.

We are so used to wearing masks that we often forget who we are. Think for a moment, how realistic is your self-image? What is your 'why' and do you have an answer to it? The answer will show whether you're true to yourself or not, and whether you are evolving or not. Having a vision is not wearing a mask but knowing and owning who you are.

Asking 'why' and expecting an answer will help you to become a better person and a true leader. Vision becomes a guide that defines our core values. Understanding those values and how to implement them is essential to living a fulfilling life.

One-size-fits-all is not an answer for strong personalities and real leaders. For visionaries, not being true to oneself is fatal. Vision helps people to connect to their true selves and become better leaders who make a positive difference for others. In other words, vision connects your inner universe with the external world.

Defining the Future

Vision aids us in defining the future. The future will come anyway but in which form depends on how we envision it and the impact it has on humanity.

This time-forward thinking is based on the ability to use the future as a point-of-reference for defining today's actions. Vision is not about the past, and surely it isn't important for those who always look backwards and are afraid to let go of the familiar. Vision involves putting one's mind in the future, imagining it and then looking back to the present to see how to get there.

One of the most prominent visionaries I ever met is David Katz. David Katz has been named one of the world's most compassionate entrepreneurs by *Salt* magazine. He is the recipient of the United Nations Lighthouse award for Planetary Health, recipient of the Paris Climate Conference Sustainia community award, the Past President of the Vancouver Chapter of the

Entrepreneurs' Organization (EO) and named an Entrepreneurs' Organization, Global Citizen.

David is also the founder and CEO of The Plastic Bank, an internationally recognised solution to ocean plastic. The Plastic Bank is the world's only organisation to monetise plastic waste. It provides incentives to the world's disadvantaged to collect and trade plastic waste as currency. The Plastic Bank solves poverty and reduces plastic waste by revealing the value in ocean-bound plastic waste.

His humanitarian work has earned him international recognition. David has been featured in hundreds of international news and investigative articles, including *Forbes*, *Time Magazine*, *Fast Company* and *National Geographic*. David can be found at TED.com, is featured in an award-winning documentary and has starred in an international reality television show.

I asked him to share how he sees the importance of vision.

'This is a cliché, but if you always do what you have always done, you will always get what you have always got. Most people believe that they are creating vision from the past but what they are doing is recreating the past. They are like hamsters in a wheel. They may not think that they are really creating vision from what they already know and that in itself is not vision but it is the past.

I would go on to argue that vision as I know it is relevant to a stay-at-home mother. It's relevant to the schoolteacher. It is the ability to live into a chosen future, from knowing nothing to contemplating the abundant and unlimited possibilities of life.

Yet vision is unavailable to most people because they are attached to their egos. It takes vulnerability and conscious decisions to truly come to an unlimited vision. Vision lives not in the past. I ask people when you think of tomorrow, what is your reference and people always say – from today? It's not vision if you take the position from today as it is only a reproduction in a different way from what you already know.

Personal life vision and business vision – they're still part of your life. It's still part of your development and part of your heritage. We have the opportunity to choose who our children's parents will be. It's the way I do everything. It's compassion and care over life, care for those who can't care for themselves. It's being a voice. It's being courageous. It's doing what we know to be right whether it's popular or leads to wealth, to be right in terms of adding value to the family. The beauty of vision is that ultimately the business vision is a vehicle of a personal life vision'.

Being too attached to the past leads to an unsatisfactory present and depressing future. It distracts and prevents people from working for something better.

Vision is like looking at the present from the future's standpoint. A visionary puts his or her own mark on the future while physically being here and now. It dictates how we care for people around us and securing not only our own but their future as well.

Life is not a place we live in but a path we take. Vision defines a path into the future where one must lead others. One must be bold enough to shift from the standpoint of the comfortable present to the unknown and the yet unexplored future and explore new horizons.

Let me introduce Adam Witty. Adam Witty is the founder and Chief Executive Officer of Advantage|ForbesBooks, which he has built into one of the largest business book publishers in America. Beginning in a spare bedroom in 2005, it now serves over 1,300 members in all 50 U.S. states and 67 countries. Advantage was listed on the Inc. 5000 list of America's most rapidly growing private companies for seven years and named in the Best Places to Work in South Carolina list for 2013, 2014, 2015 and 2017.

Most recently, Advantage has partnered with Forbes to create ForbesBooks, the first book-publishing imprint for the global media company. Launched in 2016, ForbesBooks is the next step in Forbes' 100-year history of distribution and innovation in the media business.

Adam is a sought-after speaker, teacher and consultant. He has shared the stage with Steve Forbes, Gene Simmons of KISS, Peter Guber and Bobby Bowden. Adam has been featured in *The Wall Street Journal, Investor's Business Daily, USA Today* and more.

He was named the Young Presidents' Organization 40 Under 40, 50 Most Progressive and was named to the 2011 *Inc.* magazine 30 Under 30 list of 'America's Coolest Entrepreneurs'.

'I think that vision is obviously having a view for what the future will bring. In many cases it's seeing a future that many people don't see today. It's seeing a future that is brighter than today and has more opportunity than today, and ultimately adds more value to somebody's life tomorrow than they currently are getting today. Vision is being able to see beyond the horizon and see something really great and really profound. Hence, it's very hard for people to feel and be able to visualize something that just isn't a reality.

In many ways, leaders paint that vision in deep color that is clear, that is compelling, and that is exciting, and something that they want to participate in. The really effective leaders are the ones that have the ability to paint a picture of the future that is bright and color detailed, whereas for most people it's in grainy black.

Vision is important for everything. I think having a compelling vision of the future is certainly important for a business. It's certainly important for a family. It's certainly important for your own personal life. When you don't have a compelling vision for your future then for most people they are living a life without hope for a better tomorrow. When you lose the hope for a better tomorrow, for some people it's as if they've given up their will to live, they don't have anything that they're looking forward to, and that's something that immediately will erode any happiness that you have in your life.

We have hundreds of millions of people around the world who are depressed, who are going through the motions day in and day out, who are not looking forward to tomorrow and who have no vision for what the future will be and certainly don't have a vision that the future will be better than what they have today. When you are without vision you can get yourself into a very dark place individually. When a company is without vision, it becomes stagnant, it becomes stale and it will begin to regress and slide backwards in some cases all the way into bankruptcy and the dustbin of history'.

It's very difficult for people to see a future that doesn't yet exist. It's hard to feel and visualise something that just isn't a reality. No one can create something totally new by ticking boxes off a standardised checklist. Vision is needed to construct that new and as-yet invisible reality.

Vision must be bold enough to break the old boundaries and set new ones beyond the horizon. And it only comes when you leave familiar comforts behind.

A Guide for Life and Business

Vision is a ladder a capable leader uses to reach success. Using a sports metaphor, we can say that to get from a second division to a premier league, one must have a vision as a layout for greater achievements.

I interviewed John Spence as he helps leaders of all ranks with vision and strategy development. John Spence is an exemplary achiever. At the age of 26, John was the CEO of the International Rockefeller Foundation, overseeing projects in 20 countries. Just two years later, *Inc.* Magazine named him one of America's Up and Coming Young Business Leaders. The American Management Association named John one of America's Top 50 Leaders to Watch along with Sergey Brin and Larry Page of Google and Jeff Bezos of Amazon. Today, John is one of the Top 100 business thought leaders in the world. He has built his entire career around the principle of 'Making the Very Complex. . .Awesomely Simple'.

> *'Working with businesses and individuals I found that they seem to be confused when we talk about vision, mission, values, purpose, and things like that. I've been teaching a workshop in executive level programs at Wharton, Cornell, and other universities called Strategies for Success. It's basically a strategic planning workshop for your life. In that class, I ask how many of them currently have a clear vision for their life and a written set of personal core values.*
>
> *Typically, I get about a hundred and twenty executives in all my classes and out of a hundred and twenty people in the room only one or two will have a written set of values and a vision before they get to the class. It's shocking to them to realize that they've been sort of wandering through life and that*

they understand that some of the stress they've created in their own life is because they've never actually sat down and said, what are my personal core values and what is my personal vision for my life? And it's a big shock for people in their mid-40s to mid-50s to realize they're a majority of the way into their career and have never ever done this in their life.

If you want to achieve something it must be defined in a clearly measurable way. Statements like, 'I want to be successful' or 'I want to be happy' are not visions. It must be specific.

The same is important for vision in business whether it is a small business or a major corporation. If you don't have a vividly clear, compelling, and well-communicated vision then people come to work every day and they don't know what they are supposed to do. They do the job, but don't know why or where they or the company is going.

I also believe you need a vision for your life, your family, and you need a vision for your career and business. They're obviously all intertwined. They're all aligned and mutually supportive. I should note that personal vision drives your business vision quite a bit. I strongly believe that you can't be a leader of others unless you can lead yourself first. It's hard to be visionary for your organization if you're not even visionary for yourself'.

Vision as the best life and business guide comes as a result of deep learning of self, clear understanding of goals and aims, and a strong belief in the possibility of achieving something great. It is the result of facing fears and doubts about oneself. Overcoming a sense of meaninglessness is purely an application of mind and soul that makes a human fully capable of overcoming all challenges and barriers.

Unclear goals and mere dreams don't get anyone far. This is like whispering your wishes into a fortune teller's ears. They accomplish nothing. Only clear goals inspire focused support, whereas unclear goals are like obstacles in the road.

A Means of Breaking Out from Negativity

People see the world through the lens of their own habits, preconceptions and biases that are firmly imprinted into their minds. No one can say 'no' to a non-satisfactory present and break out from it without having a vision for a different and better future.

For visionaries, creating a profoundly brighter future is a cause that is greater than anything else, worth going through all sorts of hard work, sacrifice, challenges and struggles. Their craving to create a better reality for themselves and others is exceptional despite critics and resistance.

Hence, this is still almost magic to some extent, allowing one to break boundaries and barriers with little more than sheer will. The time and energy of a visionary's desires and dreams are directed towards fulfilling the vision.

One visionary with this kind of experience is Noel Ferguson, who is the founder, Executive Director and Chairman of the Institute of One World Leadership. He is a visionary leader, commentator and author of *Manage without Mayhem, The Good Guide to Bad Management, Positive Value Leadership* and *Rocket Powered Leadership*.

Noel made his way up from the unsafe streets of Belfast to create the Institute of One World Leadership which stands for creating collaborative intelligence and positive leadership values. It is the only leadership institute with a global presence.

During his career as an executive and consultant, Noel successfully led incredible global-scale projects such as the implementation of multi-million dollar worldwide transformational change programs and interventions in thousands of locations in 140 countries.

He survived testicular cancer at 21 and today helps young leaders turn their dreams into reality. Noel is in the top 0.1% of Leadership and Management Experts on social media actively helping those younger generations achieve success.

> '*Without vision people perish. Equally it can be said that without people, a vision perishes. Without people to inspire or accept your visionary call to action, then a vision will be nothing more than a mental aspiration in your head. To me a vision is important because you want to know where you're going to end up in life which is full of so many uncertainties and complexities. You have no guarantee of reaching the destination that you want but you certainly have no chance of reaching it if you have no vision.*

It's like standing on the shore, and looking out over the sea. In the distance you see an island you want to reach, and you use your vision to imagine yourself there. You don't just jump on the first boat you find and start paddling. I've seen many leaders and companies do that. They grasp the next idea, be it a product or service, and set the company sail without thinking through the steps needed to reach the destination. The consequence is they get blown off course due to lack of planning and inadequate resources.

Critically, while a vision is an intangible, ethereal future, the steps you take personally and organisationally to reach the vision, must be considered, planned, resourced, reviewed and refined on a cyclical basis.

I've also seen organisations where the senior team doesn't agree with the organisational vision. This is how mutiny starts to develop. As the Leader, this is where your visionary leadership needs to kick in, by reinforcing your vision; but critically, you should have adequately conveyed your vision before setting sail, and tested understanding!

In terms of my personal life, vision has always been very important. For some reason, I've always been driven to do something different. I don't know whether it's because I grew up in Belfast, Northern Ireland, which was a difficult circumstance. My parents worked hard, but our financial position was meagre. My father was an unskilled worker, and I felt that my peers looked down upon me due to my personal and family circumstances.

I always felt unworthy, degraded, that no matter how hard I worked or how good a job I could do, that it would never be good enough. I've come to learn in later years that this is known as 'Imposter Syndrome'.

Despite these feelings of inadequacy, I've always had an open and questioning mind, wanting to know how things work, and why people behave as they do. My childhood and teenage years were spent growing up in the middle of Belfast, the only television news was the daily review of murders, bombs, riots, knee-cappings, that occurred across Northern Ireland during the civil war. I couldn't understand why people were killing each other because of religion. Why are we doing this? Why can't we do it a different way? It planted a seed in my childhood mind, that I wanted to make the world a better place.

That purpose remains with me; I want to leave this world a better place. I don't know where that place is. I know it's not on the visible horizon, but I'm hopeful that it's out there somewhere beyond the horizon. It's also important to recognise that you may not achieve your vision within your own lifetime, so you need to inspire others to give further life to your vision. Make your vision, become theirs.

And so, I know where I am now is not where I want to be or where I want the world to be'.

Vision is a vehicle for change while presenting a destination for those who are not satisfied with a hopeless present. It gets visionaries busy living and progressing from a black-grey-brick-dull coloured environment to a colourful future.

'Get busy living or get busy dying' is a famous line delivered by Andy Dufresne, played by Tim Robbins, and by 'Red' Redding, played by Morgan Freeman in *The Shawshank Redemption* (1994).

It is impossible to make that seemingly obvious choice without vision. Vision defines that choice, allowing one to take control knocking down barriers that reality likes to put in the way. Vision is what allowed me to change my life from hopelessness to meaningfulness and make a difference in the lives of others.

Uniting Force or Transfused Energy

Do you have a vision, or are you looking to create one? If yes, then surely you noticed how quickly doers and people with ideas surrounded you from that moment when you realised that your vision is your main driver. Your mind craves association with similar-minded people. Vision works as an ultimate uniting force that pulls people to it and towards each other.

People united around a common goal are unstoppable. They complement each other, add value to every detail while making it even greater, and thus become mutually affected. This is critically important for innovation and creating new ground-breaking products and services.

Feyzi Fatehi, the CEO of Corent Tech, is a technology visionary, inventor, innovator and entrepreneur. He is also a Silicon Valley veteran of a Fortune 100 company and multiple disruptive technology start-ups. As one of the five co-inventors of the first real-time database, Feyzi is a pioneer in inventing SaaS (Software as a Service) enabling technologies. His vision is to 'democratise SaaS'. It is a technology and enterprise software delivery and business model that is now a must-have for corporations across the globe. He was named one of 'The 30 Most Inspiring Business leaders, 2019' by *Mirror Review* and has received numerous awards, including the prestigious CODiE Lifetime Achievement Award, previously bestowed on Steve Jobs, Bill Gates and Steve Wozniak, among other visionary technology leaders.

'A powerful vision becomes a magnet and pulls everyone towards it. It becomes a unifying force for those who subscribe to it. A vivid vision becomes a longing and allows us to 'see' something that our hearts and minds desire. A key distinction between vision and mere ideas, goals, and objectives is that vision works as a magnet and 'pulls' you towards it, as opposed to others that you need to 'push' yourself to try to attain.

Vision which mostly resides in our hearts rather than in our minds allows us to see something which is not yet visible, since it hasn't been created yet. But we're creating its image in our minds and in a sense fooling our brain it is there and therefore achievable, and then we make it happen empowered by intense desire, and the longing in our hearts. As it has been said – 'Sight is a function of the eyes, but vision is a function of the heart.'

Vision is a unifying force whether in business or in personal life. Actually, the importance of vision in personal life is often ignored as we mainly focus on things we aim to achieve in business. Personal life impacts the level of your personal energy. As executives, at the end of the day, the biggest asset or maybe sometimes the only asset we have is our own positive personal energy because we put that to use and everything else stems from having that can-do, will-do, reservoir of energy capital. Our number one job is conservation of energy. That's our own energy conservation program not wasting our positive energy on trivial and non-consequential matters that are not going to make a positive difference in our lives and help us get closer to attaining our vision. We are well advised to consciously care about how we spend our energy. In this sense, I focus on energy management a lot more than time management. If I have the energy I make the time, if I have the energy I come up with ideas and that allow me to keep that big vision vivid and alive in my heart.

In my late 20s I was lucky to make it to the summit of Mount Whitney, which is the tallest mountain in the lower 48 contiguous United States. While I was a rigorous tennis player and hiker, I was in no shape to even imagine attempting to ascend to Whitney's summit at first. I hadn't even climbed a midsize mountain at that point in my life. A friend of mine,

Scott, who was a former member of the Marine Special Operation team, committed to training me. We persistently trained for three months. Both Scott and another friend, John, who was a 'rocket scientist' working for NASA and was a fitness fanatic, who later decided to join us, were in a much better shape and in the climb I asked them to forward ahead of me, while I was struggling to catch up with them in pursuit of making it to the summit. While I was completely exhausted, and out of breath, given the diluted oxygen levels at the 14K plus elevation, with a bad case of oxygen sickness, muscle pain, headache and nausea, I decided that I was done. I was just about to turn around and start descending back to the base camp when I saw a glimpse of the summit from a small opening in the clouds. As soon as I could see the summit something magic happened. I felt a surge of energy and as a result pulled myself together and a couple of hours later made it to the summit – all because that glimpse revived my vision of seeing myself standing on the summit. In overcoming a physical challenge, at least for me, a vivid, revived, perhaps re-focused vision gives me a big mental boost. It re-charges my batteries with a fresh surge of energy again and again'.

Feyzi Fatehi extends the idea of vision from being a uniting force or a magnet as he calls it to being a source of critical energy or mojo necessary for achieving what others deem impossible.

A unifying vision generates energy in each person involved, multiplying as it passes between people. A vision fires up hearts and minds with enthusiasm, anticipation and a can-do attitude. People thus inspired are not just energised, but become sources of energy for others.

On the other hand, those not subscribed to a powerful, meaningful and moving vision are often tired and exhausted. In other words, office silos are always tired and exhausted. They avoid any genuine effort to engage and only pretend or imitate involvement. They deplete, drain and diminish those around them with negativity, disbelief, indifference and self-doubt.

Therefore, a logical question arises – will you achieve that positive energy to reach the summits of success, fulfilment and happiness in your personal and business life, or are you prepared to live on the depleted energy levels of self-doubt?

A Provision for Inspiring Life

Whether in life or business, we can move as far as we can cast our thinking. Inspiration keeps our thinking hot and active. The more we move up and forward, the more we realise the need for it, at every stage of life and development. We become addicted to it. Inspiration feeds vision, which in turn, generates more inspiration.

What is the basis for an exemplary life – money, status or vision? I addressed this question to Her Excellency Ms. Sania A. Ansari, the Chairperson of Ansari Group Ltd and Consultant for Royal Office, involved in bilateral business development between multinational companies and UAE enterprises as well as the overall market development of UAE.

Ms. Ansari is globally known for her humanitarian efforts with a number of non-profit organisations, especially those focused on women, youth and refugees. She is the chairperson for the Ansari Foundation and United Refugee Green Council of Canada (URGC), Ambassador-at-Large for Global Tolerance Faces, Ambassador-at-Large for Peace and Human Rights for the International Human Rights Organization and Ambassador-at-Large for the International Human Rights Commission.

Ms. Ansari is a Member of the Who's Who Global Hall of Fame for Business Consultancy and was featured in 'The Top 100 People in Finance Magazine 2019' based in the USA.

'Vision is more like a provision. You get inspired by something or someone and then there comes in your mind that you also want to be at the same level or you also want to achieve certain things and then you start dreaming about it. When you start dreaming about something big you become very driven and you create your vision.

Then you move further and your vision becomes clearer and it becomes a clear plan for the future. This is how I want to be in the future, for my whole life. It is for career, for relationships, and for every aspect of our life.

From a career perspective, you have to have a clear vision because you want to know which direction you're heading and if you don't have a vision you will be lost without any idea how to proceed further.

If we think about leadership, you can only become a true leader by being a visionary and being a respectful member in a society. If you have money but no vision, then you're just a guy with money.
From the personal life standpoint, I am willing to change things for the better and set myself a big goal. It is a step for the betterment of my life. When you have a vision, it becomes your lifestyle or the way you want to live your life and achieve certain milestones'.

Having a generous attitude whether in personal life or business while believing in tomorrow is the simple recipe of those who know the path to a successful future. They are full of optimism, which leads them to greater achievements.

All people need dopamine and serotonin, the so-called 'hormones of happiness', and some people need adrenalin to energise their life. Visionaries have vision that gives them dopamine, serotonin, noradrenalin, adrenalin and other neuro-mediators that make their life not easy but enjoyable.

The stories of those who went from rags to riches are reflections of their vision. Vision allowed them to turn a dream into a reality. They are not the smartest, but they didn't surrender to a prescribed or programmed life but desired a reality they couldn't yet see, making themselves the CEOs of their own lives.

It wouldn't be correct to say that vision makes people happy, but vision leads people to much happier, energised, inspired and satisfied lives. For visionaries, it is a lifestyle that turns day-to-day boredom into a top-of-the-world life regardless of whatever difficulties and challenges might come.

Differentiating True Leaders from Bad Leaders

Vision is more important than we think. Whether in personal life or in business, a compelling vision pulls all goals and desires together. True vision also helps to balance your business and personal life. Vision is a concentration of human desires and an unwavering decision to live a valuable and meaningful life. It is a foundation for life planning allowing one to build something solid and be proud of. To do something really valuable and important, one must have vision.

In terms of personal life, no one can define a reason for your presence on Earth and the way you live it except you. Aimless and meaningless goals lead you nowhere except to regret for a wasted life.

Your vision should have a name, simple and straightforward. This will help define your vision. It is important to consider that nothing is guaranteed in this life. Vision also doesn't guarantee anything, but it does change the rules.

From a business standpoint, having a vivid and compelling vision regardless of its scale is what differentiates true leaders and bad leaders. How to ensure that a business will have a few million dollars revenue? The answer is simple – entrust a billion dollars to a person without vision. It would not take long to become a 'millionaire'.

Vision is the foundation of everything. Vision comes first and strategy comes next, and not vice versa. Can you imagine a groundbreaking innovation without vision? The answer is very obvious.

Practical Tips

- Too many people live in the past, some stay in the present and a few live in the future. Vision is a path to the future that no one can override or overrule. This is a path accessible only to those prepared to think beyond the present. Where are your thoughts?
- Write down why vision is important to you. Do you have a vision for personal life? Do you have a vision for business or your career? Write these answers down and evaluate how compelling and interlinked they are.
- Be prepared to challenge yourself as all visionaries do. Otherwise, simply put this book down or give it to somebody for whom this really matters.

2

What Lies Behind
the 'Aha' Moment

'Imagination is the beginning of creation. You imagine what you
desire, you will what you imagine, and at last, you create what
you will'.

George Bernard Shaw

Giving It a Name

Vision is a masterpiece born of the mind that shapes the lives
of many in the physical world. It is born in the mind or
minds of the masters of thinking who use human desires and
existing possibilities to create it. Every visionary defines vision in
a unique way. Here are just a handful of examples of how visionaries define what vision is. s a critical element on which ideas are
often built

'A successful vision is the translation of a positive image for the future
into reality'.

Marshall Goldsmith

'Vision is a reality fully executed, in which I use my words to invite people
to actively participate. It's a place of being. It's a reality'.

David Katz, Founder and CEO of Plastic Bank

'It's a describable state of your being and why you exist'.
Garry Ridge, Chairman and CEO, WD-40 Company

'Vision is a persuasive and motivational image of the future which people sign up for'.
Stuart Crainer, Co-founder, Thinkers50

'Vision is an aspiration for an organization or a group of people that is believable, that drives the behavior and choices of that organization to actually maximize the chance of creating that aspirational reality'.
Asheesh Advani, President and CEO of Junior Achievement (JA) Worldwide

'Vision is an ability to tap the future with a tangible solution. This is the inner sight that allows me to envision, create and translate it into what I am prepared to do for others'.
Raphael Louis, Leader and President of the National Coalition Party of Canada (NCPC)

'Vision is seeing a tomorrow that is more exciting, more prosperous, more motivating than what you have today and seeing beyond in realistic and tangible ways'.
Adam Witty, Founder and CEO of Advantage Media/ForbesBooks

'Vision is a desired positive future state which you want to achieve'.
Noel Ferguson, Founder and Executive Chairman of Institute of One World Leadership (IOWL)

All these definitions reflect the visionaries' strong desire to create a reality that will change the future.

Vision is a future reality created today for the benefit of others. It is the most versatile means of shaping the future. On one hand, a vision is a future reality we foresee and strive to build. On the other hand, it is a disruptive force that allows a higher stage of satisfaction by creating something real and practically useful for many people.

Vision is not about waiting for the right moment. It is about creating that moment in advance and surprising the heavens. You have a vision, a picture of a better reality that you can help bring about. What are you waiting for?

A Truth Behind the 'Aha' Moment

Does vision come as a sensation, or gift, or is it the result of hard work? This is a question commonly asked at every conference I participate in on vision and every lecture on leadership at business schools. To answer it, we need to learn how the vision is born, how we arrive at the 'aha' moment.

In 1869, Dmitri Mendeleev, a Russian chemist not very well-known at that time, devised the periodic table, which is still considered to be the most comprehensive system for classifying the chemical elements. We all spent hours looking at it in chemistry classes. Mendeleev offered his compelling and straightforward framework for classifying chemical elements by their atomic mass and common properties. He also predicted characteristics of elements which were not even known at that time.

It is commonly known that the vision of the periodic table came to him while asleep. He shared this story as a miraculous tale of someone gifted from the heavens. In fact, Mendeleev worked hard for eighteen years looking for simple solutions to complicated issues. For the two years prior to the discovery, he worked tirelessly aiming to deliver his 'Principles of Chemistry'. On February 17, 1869, he was so deeply immersed in finding the solution for three days and nights that he even forgot about a train that he was supposed to catch that morning. After these draining three days, he fell asleep and. . . Mendeleev wrote later that in a dream he envisioned a table where all chemical elements fell into place as required. He woke up shocked and thrilled and put this discovery on paper, and his name into history.

Mendeleev's story from the nineteenth century seemingly shows that a miracle stands on the ground of hard work. How true this is in today's terms?

David Katz was looking for a solution to the problem of plastic waste in the world's oceans. It took more than thirty-five years before he found an effective one. Today, his Plastic Bank helps to save the planet, help the poor and turn plastic into a new form of currency. Plastic Bank, a social enterprise from Canada, is monetising plastic through recycling collected ocean plastic waste while empowering those most affected by the waste. It works to prevent plastic waste from entering oceans by incentivising people in developing countries to collect plastic from their communities in exchange for cash or goods and services – be it food, clean water or school tuition for their children.

'It's been my life time growing up on an island on the west coast of Canada and even from my childhood from 35 years ago when I was a teenager beginning to witness plastic washing up on my beaches. At first, I thought oh how fascinating something washing up from some distant land, or, how amazing where did it come from. Then over the course of time to see this wave of plastic approaching and recognizing early that it was garbage – other people's waste – and then whenever I travelled it became a part of my context. That context entered my paradigm. It appeared louder and louder in the pictures that I saw and I couldn't help but be moved by seeing images of the dead albatross on Midway Island, the turtles' corpses, something that sticks with me all the time.

It's horrible. But what's relevant there? It is that the plastic will a hundred times outlive the decomposing corpse of the animal it kills and be free to continue murdering. It doesn't just murder once. It is a killing machine as it drifts; it is a disaster.

I've been looking for a solution for my whole life. I'd seen something needed to be done. I didn't know it was going to be me. I was just looking for a solution.

I attended an event in Silicon Valley called Singularity University. At that event they had the greatest emerging technologies. They were discussing what they call the global grand challenges like malnutrition. What's a grand challenge for humanity? They never discussed plastic, but I knew that it was of course a global grand challenge before people were aware.

One of the training seminars was about 3D printing or what really additive manufacturing is and the person that was conducting the seminar had a brown belt. That it was one solid piece of 3D printed manufacturing was fascinating. It was manufactured from one solid long strand of thin filament plastic and a nozzle moving in the necessary pattern.

I asked how much the belt sold for. $80 was the answer. How much did the material cost? $10.

It was in that moment I recognized the only thing that provided the value of the material was its shape. They took plastic that was $10, changed its shape and added $70 of value. That was the nucleus to the Plastic Bank.

If we no longer saw the bottle as waste but as money then that could be the beginning of change. The same volume of plastic that goes into a car part that could sell for $200 is the same plastic volume that goes into bottling. Something that is free on the street with a changed form could be hundreds of dollars in the store.

How might we then change the way that we perceive the value of the material? What if all plastic was money for the world? Would that be an origin of change?

I remember this day perfectly well, May the 11th, 2013. It was a moment from where I created the vision that we should create a currency for the world, a recognizable and tradable currency as a new form of money. In this sense, plastic is exchanged for some kind of money which can be reproduced again and be useful for people and make a positive change as well. Today, we're the world's largest chain of stores for the poor where everything in the store can be purchased using plastic garbage. Everything from school tuition, to medical insurance, to pharmaceuticals, to Wi-Fi, to cooking fuel, and everything the poor need. We're like bank branches in which people deposit plastic garbage by mass and withdraw cash through a digital wallet to pay for the things that they and their children need'.

Vision is a response to the most critical problems and issues that people face. It releases our inner abilities. Realistically, this is a practical, pragmatic and realistic reflection of our dreams and long-term desires, and a plan to make them reality. From the moment when thoughts come together and offer a solution, a vision defines the world around us. Vision doesn't come overnight but as a result of years of focused thinking looking for a solution to a serious challenge.

Another fascinating story comes from Feyzi Fatehi, CEO of Corent Tech. His long journey to vision and success is another example that vision doesn't come easy. It takes years of hard work and countless sleepless nights.

'I was in my mid-20s when HP hired me from college. They assigned me to a team of two other people. I was number three and later our team became five people and I have to say, every single one of them was a lot smarter than I was.

Together we invented the fastest database in the world. Our goal was to make it 10 times faster than the leading commercial databases at the time such as Oracle. But we were young and naïve. We exceeded that 10× goal and we came up with a database that was about 1,000 times faster than the leading databases at the time. Our invention was announced in June 1989 via a detailed write-up at the prestigious HP Journal, the official publication of HP Labs in Palo Alto. It was not long after the Chernobyl nuclear meltdown tragedy had happened. A reporter who covered the HP Real-Time Database Management System (HP RTDBMS as we called it) said 'if the Chernobyl powerplant had had access to this database it could have prevented the meltdown'.

That commentary brought it all together for me. Technology innovation to save lives and make the world a better place became a lot more palpable, tangible, and meaningful to me. It hit home that all these late nights, staying up thinking, or waking up in the middle of the night having an epiphany about a new design approach, were not just some theoretical R&D type of work but they could actually lead to a consequential, real-life breakthrough. As a result, I was further inspired and energized by the idea of pursuing a career in inventing disruptive technology and innovation.

The success of the project emboldened me. I started writing about it and speaking at different conferences. One of them earned me the recognition as the best speaker of a key international technology conference, and so on, and as a 20-something technologist I was encouraged by that early success, that also earned me my first official invention patent.

Fast forward, in March 2001, I was invited to give the keynote at the first Pan-European Cloud and SaaS Conference at Cavalieri Waldorf Astoria Hotel in Rome. The terms Cloud and SaaS had not been coined yet. Up till then, they were called something like 'hosting' and ASP

(Application Service Provider) which was like the grandparent of today's Cloud and SaaS technologies. At the time, it was a very arduous, very inefficient process to offer a software application as a service in an efficient and scalable way. How can we take that wasteful repetition of reinventing the wheel by thousands of companies in the world and turn it into a service that is centrally delivered? The aim was to build a solution that allowed everybody to use it without installing, upgrading, and maintaining it one customer at a time.

In other words, how could we turn the software applications that every company has to download and install, manage and upgrade into a service they'd receive over the internet? Meaning one enterprise software instance that can have tens of thousands of companies and therefore larger number of users that can subscribe to it, but with every company maintaining the integrity of their own data, their own workflows, their own rules, and their own customization. Then again, there is one software application that is being efficiently managed. Imagine there is one power plant that generates and transmits power but somebody needs 100 volts and somebody needs 220 volts. Somebody needs different amperage to charge their electric automobile. How could you get the same power plant sending the same generated power and then it's transformed for different usage and purposes accordingly instead of having separate generators, and transmission lines and cables for each type of power usage!

To get the point across in layman's terms, we used a common real estate term called multi-tenancy. This is like in a New York skyscraper with fifty floors and each floor having ten independent apartments totalling five hundred independent units. So compare it with a single-family mansion built on the same block on a similar size lot of land. Then an architect says that she can take this land and build a fifty-storey building and each floor could have several apartment units. We did something similar within the software industry.

Corent Tech's platform transforms a single software application designed for use by a single company into 'an apartment high-rise' that never runs out of apartment units to rent and the cost of each new apartment to the landlord (the SaaS provider) would approach zero. That's the invention and we have 83 patent claims granted for the invention so far. It took us only fifteen years to make it simple, intuitive, and easy to use without deep training and expertise.

Our 'vision' was to deliver SaaS in an absolute cost-effective way and instead of spending years of programming, do it in hours or days, and that vision has become a reality today. That is why some people have said what Corent's team has done is the first-ever major disruption in the history of the software industry – turning software into a service without a single line of programming.

Salesforce.com became a company that made the number one SaaS solution in the world, because of the vision of its founder, Marc Benioff. Then there was a handful of others that created successful, efficient, and scalable SaaS solutions and then there are thousands of other companies that we call pseudo-SaaS providers. They were not able to deliver their SaaS offering in an efficient and scalable way. That's why one of them after $380M of funds raised just went bankrupt and another one after $120M couldn't sustain themselves, because while they delivered their offering as a subscription service, they couldn't sustain their high cost of service delivery due to their inherent technological inefficiencies. The subscription fees the customers were willing to pay them were less than the cost of delivering their service. That is why California Business Journal in the cover story of their July 2019 issue titled "Democratizing SaaS," said "While Salesforce.com is known for 'legitimizing' SaaS, Corent is getting recognized for 'democratizing' SaaS!," again a testimony to the power of a clear, concise, and compelling vision'.

Finding the simplest possible solution and making the unaffordable affordable to millions of users is a great challenge. Feyzi Fatehi's story is an excellent example of it. His vision is finding the smartest and simplest way of making complex products into a cost-effective and efficiently deliverable service and it is certainly not a simple and easy task.

None of the visionaries I know in person or through studying different cases or by learning about historical personalities received their vision as a gift. The elaborated vision demands years of looking for the best solution. It takes even more effort to ensure it has an impact.

Through long-term effort and sincere devotion to finding a solution to a complicated problem, visionaries pull together all their ideas and desires. They mobilise all their senses and resources. They concentrate everything into something big and make the best use of it. This is what counts when we talk about a vision's creation.

Imagination Is the Mother of Vision

If we can imagine something in real terms then we can make it real. The more precise and greater the imagination, the greater the achievement. It is imagination that makes us mighty and casts our minds into the future. Albert Einstein in his interview published in *The Saturday Evening Post* in 1929 was asked, 'Then you trust more to your imagination than to your knowledge?' He responded – 'I am enough of the artist to draw freely upon my imagination. Imagination is more important than knowledge. Knowledge is limited. Imagination encircles the world'.

Imagination is the mother of vision. Starting with often unclear signs it grows into something real, strong and compelling. The process of turning imagination into a strong vision can be envisioned in three parts – larva, cocoon and fully shaped adult butterfly.

Larva

A larva primarily does one thing – it eats and eats and eats. A vision in the larva stage uses our knowledge base to grow. We cannot see this process, but it goes on in the back of our mind, usually without our knowing it. It is fed by our knowledge, conscious and unconscious reactions, feelings and emotions, dreams and responses to different challenges.

At the larval stage, we reveal our imaginative and creative inner child. This is where children are strong and adults tend to miss most opportunities. Children see beauty where we feel lost. Most adults train themselves to ignore a great deal of information, often to their detriment.

Imagination is wild and crosses all possible boundaries. Hence, we often dismiss this force by saying to ourselves something like, 'you are not serious', 'you should think like a grown person', 'it is too funny to be valuable', and so on.

Even if the first thoughts about how to solve a problem are not strong or efficient, they are still very valuable. They often trigger the formation of a vision.

We are consciously restricting our imagination. At the very first stage, 99.99% of brilliant ideas are killed by those who are supposed to nurture and grow them – 'this is not good enough to take seriously', 'I am too busy with serious things today to worry about tomorrow', 'tomorrow is too distant'.

Imagination is a form of thinking that often seems risky and unusual. In reality, the risk is something we give far too much credence. Think for a moment, how many brilliant ideas you have killed while being 'too adult'?

Cocoon

Vision appears with the first gentle timid signs and often disappears from sight for some time until something reveals its presence. It may seem to not be developing at all, but big changes are happening in its subconscious. It accumulates enormous inner energy and defines the shape of that future butterfly. Very often, we simply don't notice this cocoon because of our daily concerns.

This is where a butterfly gets ready to burst out of its cocoon. The longer we ignore or deny its existence, the longer the hatching process.

No one throws away golden nuggets regardless of their size. Can you afford to miss ideas that may change your life or business? The effect of any idea is impossible to predict. Even the smallest one can grow into a world-changing vision.

Instead of wrangling with ideas, I write them down into a separate file that is revisited regularly. It helps to preserve and track them, and use them when the time comes.

Beautiful Butterfly

Vision grows into its shape fed by imagination, nurtured by inspiration and driven by a desire to solve a serious problem for the sake of others. At this stage, thoughts about it tend to wake a visionary up in the middle of the night because they are constantly working, even when asleep.

Grow beautiful and compelling ideas that can't be ignored or restricted. Even so, whether a given butterfly will live and fly or not completely depends on its creator's aims, abilities and competencies to nurture it. At this stage, we can clearly envision what the vision will become.

It can be very different from the initial idea but it is beautiful in its own way. It becomes not just productive, but reproductive as the results inspire new ideas to nurture.

Must Do for a Vision to Grow

An initial idea about a potential solution to a problem is something of a gift, but it can take years of effort to grow that first seed.

Creation of real vision is challenging and demands conscious awareness of higher purpose. Conscious awareness isn't about platitudes like, 'I have a calling' or 'taking a chance', but about consciously understanding why a certain problem should be solved. This is about a fully formed and defined 'why'.

We can get a vision of something that we are most concerned about. How great is this problem that one is prepared to devote one's own life to solve it for the benefit of many? This 'why' is the pain of others that will not let the visionary rest. Others may not see this problem or simply tolerate it like lambs but the one who does see it will make a difference in the end.

Conscious awareness sets the need to emphasise six other critical terms of vision development – constant learning, listening, scanning the environment, broad outlook, killing ego, bold thinking and intuition.

Learning

Vision demands an immediacy of thought that is rooted in constant learning. Developing vision means creating a new system of values, relationships, interdependencies and processes. This is where lessons and experiences of those with greater knowledge is much needed. Are you prepared to go back to school? Visionaries do. They learn as they breathe. They constantly learn from each other.

Garry Ridge, Chairman and CEO of WD-40 went to school already a mature leader on a global scale.

> *'Back in 1999 just after becoming the president and CEO of WD-40 Company I went back to school and I did a master's degree in leadership at the University of San Diego. The first class in that program is really about understanding who you are, and we talked a lot about vision and values at that time. That's when I really was thinking deeply about my vision.*
>
> *As I went through that two-years master's program I started my relationship with Ken Blanchard, Marshall Goldsmith and others who are not necessarily practitioners, but great thinkers. I realized that we only had time, talent, and treasure, and none of them were abundant and the more focused we were around how we were going to allocate our time, how we were going to allocate a talent, the more treasure we would have to allocate. It was kind of like one of those aha moments'.*

Learning to think from the best helps clearly define ideas and turn them into something valuable. How to ask questions beyond convenience or common understanding, how to get out of the mental comfort zone, how to grow consistently – this is where lessons from experts are much needed.

Listening

Listening to people with great attention is pragmatic. It has a twofold role. The first one is to learn about pain, desires and the long-term plans of others. Listening is a prerequisite of productive dialogue that leads to achieving a pragmatic and valuable result.

The second is to receive feedback as a tool to keep you moving in the right direction. Feedback is valuable for those who know where they are going and every suggestion that keeps them on track is invaluable.

I posed this question to Alex Goryachev who believes in listening to diverse opinions as the most critical factor in shaping the vision and strategy for innovative organisations. Alex Goryachev is Managing Director of Cisco's Co-Innovation Centers and a *Wall Street Journal* bestselling author of *Fearless Innovation*. He leads a global network of fourteen Co-Innovation Centers in North and South America, Europe, the Middle East and Asia, enabling the company's innovation ecosystem, as well as a corporate-wide portfolio of employee innovation programs. His ecosystem programs have contributed nearly $1 billion towards revenue by leveraging the network with the Internet of Things, cyber security, blockchain, artificial intelligence and 5G, generating dozens of digital solutions accelerating growth across multiple industries.

'Creating true organizational vision requires listening to a diverse range of opinions from a diverse range of stakeholders – local communities, customers, partners, employees, as well as competitors. The key to taking the first step is letting go of your ego, being transparent about your aspirations and being open to challenging feedback. True vision must be both honest and pragmatic, and too often I see organizations confusing their true goals and aspirations with PR slogans and brand messages. For example, many companies, and particularly start-ups don't often acknowledge that they must generate revenue, deliver shareholder value and profits and often mask it with vague statements. That confuses employees and ultimately does a disservice to workers and investors.

So, we must be honest, transparent and pragmatic about our aspirations – that's the only way to succeed. We must be inclusive. We must be diverse. And we must listen to others'.

Listening to people carefully means appreciating their experience. Our eyes open much by listening to different people. Only by listening can we find what worries people most and for what kind of problems a solution should be found.

Just as if we don't listen to our dearest in our personal lives, we make unrepairable cracks in family relations; if we don't talk to existing or potential customers, we create a gap between business and people. In both cases, in personal and business life we ruin everything by not listening.

In practical terms, I saw many start-ups which were stuck on their ideas, ignoring market reality. They never talked to potential customers. They were simply focused on their ideas while lacking actual vision. In fact, mature companies often fall into the same trap. They assume that they can conquer the world by looking through the window without hearing people's actual needs.

Killing Ego

Vision is a process directed towards helping others, often at the cost of one's own ego. This is a fight in which visionary leaders much prevail again and again.

A visionary unconsciously realises that if he or she wouldn't step on his own ego's throat, then there is no chance for a vision to grow. Vision and ego can't live together.

Vision is sacrificing one's self for others. This is a great gesture of giving that is based on empathy, extraordinary effort and care for others. A positive vision provides a purposeful service to others and values self-sacrifice over ego and selfishness. It attracts people and opens their hearts.

A big ego kills vision instantly. Ego is a mask that blocks out the world in favour of personal interest. It blocks everything, allowing only 'me' to grow like a balloon that will burst in sadness in the end. Have you ever been attracted by someone's ego?

In reality, we all have a reasonable dose of ego but too much turns people away and ruins opportunities for creating vision. At the same time, squeezing ego out, even drop by drop, is a hard but necessary task that results in freeing the mind and soul.

Bold Thinking

Setting out to create something with little to no resources is an act of great courage and faith. We know that today's giants, Google, Microsoft, Apple and many others were started in garages, sheds and spare bedrooms. Their vision and bold thinking were the main force behind their success.

Dr. Babalola Omoniyi started the Pan African Leadership and Entrepreneurship Development Centre (PALEDEC) in a spare bedroom as well. Dr. Babalola's story is a fascinating example of bold thinking and creating something big while having very little at hand.

'Everything started in 2014. I had just resigned from a journalist position in a Nigerian magazine company. I knew that there was something bigger than just what I wanted. Something bigger than me.

My idea was to rewrite the story of Africa and connect Africa to the world. We want to present Africa as a continent that anybody in the world can come to and invest in and prosper.

The project that started in my spare bedroom as FBI Africa Magazine quickly turned into the Pan-African Leadership and Entrepreneurship Development Centre and the Pan-African Humanitarian Summit that we do every year in different places such as Ghana, UAE, Morocco, Tanzania, and Qatar. The project that started with almost no money helped to attract millions of investments from different institutional and private investors whose money helped to make a real difference for people in eighteen African countries and counting'.

Those who are risk averse are always fearful of leaving their comfort zone. They are afraid to even imagine themselves in a new reality, blocked by fear of what's going to happen and how they will cope with it.

No one can unwrap a new reality without bold thinking and accepting risk; this is not a Christmas gift. Bold thinking is a property of explorers who are very curious about what lies beyond traditional understanding and prescribed expectations while being brave enough to accept those answers. They ask questions beyond convenience or comfortable understanding. Concern over the available resources becomes secondary.

Scanning Environment

As one is attempting to impact something as big as the surrounding environment or even the entire world, it is critical to learn everything about that environment. The more you know about the world around, the more you get attuned to it, and mentally and emotionally attached to it. At the same time, it is important to consider that to evolve with the world one must be present in its reality, not distant from it. In other words, learn all the rules of the game and players first before you try to change them.

Self-awareness is critical for everyone. In this sense, if we don't know the world around us, then we can't define who we are in this world. By observing and scanning the world, we observe ourselves.

Some people see the world as a bit scary – too big, too dangerous, too unpredictable, too unmanageable. But when we know something really well, then it doesn't look unmanageable and it reveals its potential opportunities. The world is very friendly and open to those who know it.

The picture of the world is changing all the time and mindful analysis demands the mobilisation of all senses. Every little change teaches a lesson. The more you observe, the more developed your senses become, and the better human you become.

By knowing the environment, you will appreciate what it has to offer. Your environment has all the answers – just be ready and keep your eyes and ears open.

Broad Outlook

An in-depth outlook underlies a system of thinking that allows seeing deep meaning behind events. This is not about being good at solving crosswords and using those buzzwords in Friday's evening conversations by the bar. This is about understanding the nature of things and the ability to connect them against a backdrop of a million non-relevant facts.

Such an outlook allows for a clear and consistent individually composed system of knowledge that is meticulously collected and analysed over the years. A mind with a broad outlook offers the needed answers with the accompanying systematic comments on demand. These answers are often lurking in our subconscious, formed over years of learning, observing and reflecting.

At the same time, a visionary outlook appreciates the knowledge and experience of previous generations and allows access to the answers from this bottomless pool of wisdom. Being smart doesn't mean that one will become wise. A broad outlook more certainly leads to the wisdom necessary for creating a strong vision.

Intuition and Resonance

Illusion is like a morning mist that comes from nowhere and disappears to nowhere with the first bright rays of sunshine. It comes without hard thinking and disappears with the first clear thoughts about what underlies it. The reason is simple – illusion is not attached to reality and only tricks the mind.

Human intuition or instinct is something very different from illusion. It is rooted in our perception of the world and attaches our souls and unconscious minds to the universe. This is something that is very difficult to explain but extremely powerful if well developed. A gut feeling is very real and helps us to make the right choice even in very unclear situations.

This is where women-visionaries are particularly strong. I turned my questions about what is needed to create vision to Olga Uskova, President and Founder of the Cognitive Technologies Group of companies. Olga runs businesses across Russia, multiple European countries, the United States and Asia. She is also known as one of the top female IT visionaries. She was the one who facilitated the agreement on OCR and ECM solutions between Cognitive Technologies and the world's top IT-giants such as HP, Canon, Epson, IBM, Oracle and others.

Olga is the initiator and pioneer of driverless technologies in Russia, founder and main stakeholder of the Cognitive Pilot – an AI-based multi-platform autonomous driving system for ground transport and agricultural machinery. Headed by Olga, Cognitive Technologies has become one of the top international software developers of intelligent systems for autonomous driving and smart-cities technologies.

'A visionary creates a new entity or new essence in a revolutionary way and as a result this new essence resonates with the Universe.

If one doesn't resonate with the universe, he stops. Resonance is a very deep inner perception. This is getting into the rhythm of the universe. Look at Da Vinci's Mona Lisa. There is no need to analyze Mona Lisa as it is resonance and perception itself.

The same happens in business or any other areas of human action. Regardless of what we do, one makes oneself an instrument. He or she works hard and fully focuses on something important and thus, converts himself into an instrument of the Universe.

Resonance is when you and what you do get into a rhythm with the universe and this feeling or perception allows you to jump into something great. A visionary becomes a mind reader of the universe who feels and reads its intentions.

It might be a small detail to get into that resonance but not many are prepared to listen to their gut's inner radar and become that instrument of translating the universe's signals'.

The future doesn't send an email to anyone with clear plans. What it does, it sends vibes to the minds and souls of those who are tuned to the right frequency and prepared to translate these signals to others.

Our understanding of tomorrow is superficial to a great extent and can't be fully grasped by simple logic. It lies beyond the convenient logic of today. A visionary fully realises this fact and listens to his gut. The future talks to those who are prepared to listen and rewards them with great vision.

This almost animal perception is a critical element on which ideas are often built initially, and no profound vision can be created without it.

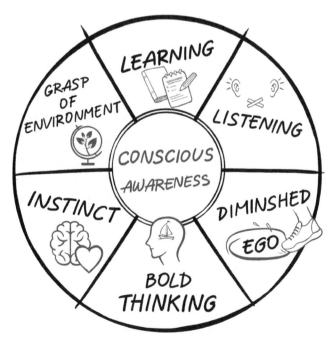

Figure 2.1 Vision creation.

To wrap up this discussion, a strong and scalable vision comes when a conscious awareness about the problem breaks through as a result of long thinking about it, or conscious awareness of a problem reaches its peak, and is well supported by learning, listening, broad outlook, instinct, diminished ego, bold thinking and a full grasp of the environment.

Conclusion

Vision is not a gift but a reward for those who are prepared to work hard solving problems that they identify along the way. It is very different from something quickly sketched on a board table as a vision statement.

I will offer a simple example. Think of a twenty-five-year business plan. Usually businesses put on paper where they want to be in twenty-five years, which is more of a goal than a plan. Visionaries talk about the next generations and our impact on them in twenty-five years' time. Can you feel a difference?

Practical Tips

- Have you ever noticed that visionaries are very optimistic? Optimism is critical for creating a vision as it adds energy during this long journey. It feeds courage, confidence and hope.
- Creating vision is a reinvention of one's self again and again. This is hard work that not many are prepared to do.
- Visionaries carry a whole world inside them and then share it with others unconditionally.
- Vision doesn't tolerate a rush but demands consistency, patience, persistence and action over the long term.
- Attune yourself to the positive model of the future, not something that sucks your time and energy like meaningless gossip, fake news and abusive negativity and the world will reveal its beauties and wonders.

3

Fighting Anti-Visionary Me

'We make a living by what we get, but we make a life by what we give'.

Winston Churchill

Vision is a living creature created in the mind. It is meant to be materialised into something very real and practical in the course of its life.

As with any living creature, vision listens and talks, and actively interacts with people. It communicates to people of all cultures, all backgrounds. It calls us to action. There is no such thing as a vision that leaves you sitting where you are.

Vision has enemies it must constantly combat. Typically, we think of vision only having external enemies, those who would get in the way of it and try to sabotage it. We tend to ignore another possibility, that we are the worst enemy of our own vision.

The reason behind this assumption is simple – we are not prepared to accept our own weaknesses and look for someone or something beyond our control to blame. In reality, the main enemies of vision reside in us.

Negativity, lack of confidence, detachment from reality, too much comfort, ego and other anti-vision forces threaten to kill vision before it is fully formed.

We often are not prepared to be seen as different, unusual. It's in our DNA to want to conform. But we also have our free will to choose who we want to be and what we want to create. Strict conformity in all ways at all times prevents us from being who we truly are. It is about being a whole personality. Not perfect, but solid and whole.

Creating a vision is a pivotal moment when one decides to look at the world differently, aiming to change it for good. Without those willing to enact their vision, we would still be living in caves.

Negativity

The first anti-vision forces are negativity and pessimism that are fed by doubts and unnecessary worries. This force is backed up by contentment and mediocrity. Some of these forces come from previous negative experiences of dealing with toxic people who left horrible scars, some are made up by ourselves, some are insistently nurtured in us by friends and relatives who don't have any ambitions, are not willing to succeed and live without any vision themselves.

People tend to pass their mistakes and negative experiences to others whether intentionally or not. They are often threatened by the success of others, thinking it a reflection of their failures. Don't surround yourself with people who have such a mind-set. Don't allow anyone to talk you into failure.

Lack of Confidence and Enthusiasm

If you don't believe in yourself, then who will believe in you? If you are not enthusiastic about your own endeavours, then who else will be? Lack of confidence only causes distraction and more doubts, leaving no chance for being focused on something greater than the usual routine. This will kill your passion which in turn will kill your vision.

If the inner you is prepared to fight for that long-nurtured vision, then you will realise how strong you are. Vision is given to you because you are fully capable, mentally and psychologically, of standing for it. Otherwise, you wouldn't be having it.

Think for a moment, you already created or are in the process of creating a life-changing vision that others only dream about. You are obliged by definition to keep going and keep creating. Be proud of yourself and your confidence will grow naturally.

Detachment from Reality

Another anti-vision force is detachment from reality. There is nothing extremely complicated about defeating this particular vision killer. It needs nothing more than constant evaluation of the environment and how your vision fits into it. Below are two very practical and real-time time opinions of experts who know how to outfight this vision destroyer.

I posed my question on how detachment impacts vision to Asheesh Advani, President and CEO of Junior Achievement (JA) Worldwide, a global NGO that creates, develops and implements hands-on educational programmes and experiences related to entrepreneurship, work readiness and financial literacy. With a network of teams in 118 countries, JA now serves over 12 million young people annually. JA implements programmes and learning experiences through partnerships with the public and private sector, including over 450,000 volunteers and 3,500 employees worldwide. In 2020, JA Worldwide was selected as one of the Top 100 NGOs in the World by NGO Advisor, ranking #7 on the list.

Asheesh Advani came up with three critically important constraints to keep vision relevant to present and forthcoming realities.

'I would emphasize three constraints which must be considered. You must watch out for financial trends which work against your vision. In other words, if your vision is to become the best organization in the world that makes horse carriages and all of a sudden everybody's driving cars, your vision is not sustainable. There's a financial reality.

The second constraint is an organizational constraint. Let's assume that your vision is to become the best electric car manufacturer in the world, but your company is tied to a legacy business and organizational structure that makes fuel-powered cars. So you theoretically are picking something which is consistent with trends but your organizational structure might get in the way of transformation no matter how much of a courageous visionary leader you are. It might be better to buy an electric car company rather than try to change your legacy organization with a bold vision.

The third constraint is that the vision that you've picked is too aspirational and too far away from reality. For example, if you want to develop the world's first blood test to get insights about a person through a drop of blood and it takes decades to develop a product which people expect in two years that could get in the way of a vision being successful. Vision must be both aspirational and realistic. People will stop believing in the vision if it is not achievable in the first five or ten years'.

In his response to this question, John Spence linked the importance of environment scanning and competence growth.

'Not scanning the environment and paying attention to what is happening around the company leaves one ignorant of reality. When this happens, we tend to hold on to what worked in the past and the vision can become unrealistically inflexible and doesn't call for a positive change. If I am building a vision without looking around and hardly understand how my vision fits into the marketplace, that lack of focus causes indifference within the organization and reluctance to try new things.

However, if I the leader has created a bold, reality-based vision for change and growth, there are sometimes people who can't skill up fast enough to get the company to the next level of development. They don't understand how different it is to run a three-billion-dollar company than a five-hundred-million-dollar company. The organization has risen to the maximum level of incompetence, it is growing faster than their people can and if they try to go any further with those folks on the team, it's going to hurt the company. To achieve the vision the leader must be willing to find ways to replace mediocrity and incompetence with people who have skills, experience, and drive to move the organization forward'.

Those two seemingly different comments are united in that withstanding this vision killer demands daily work. It is a skill that can be developed and pays off in an increased ability to predict and adapt to trends.

Ego

We already discussed the negative role of ego in the previous chapters. It bears further discussion here.

There are two constantly competing forces – vision and ego. Consider for a moment what you are building for the future and what cause you are prepared to serve for the rest of your life? Which will win is your decision.

If you are still struggling with the answer, realise no one will invest in your ego. Vision attracts those who are inspired by it and will invest to help make it a reality. Ego will make you blind, whereas a realised vision is something to be always proud of.

Ego feeds another anti-vision force, comfort, which we will discuss next.

Comfort

The desire for mental comfort blocks personal and professional growth. Comfort is a swamp that destroys a person's will. This is a force that is difficult to defeat. It always presents new excuses and reasons why you shouldn't act on your vision.

In practice, many leaders think 'I do well enough and don't need to do better' without even trying to leave their comfort zone. This leads to short-term thinking and the eventual destruction of whatever they might have accomplished.

Short-term thinking is only focused on immediate gain and instant gratification. If those gains don't come quickly enough, they substitute mission for vision, changing it loses all impact. It becomes like a malfunctioning navigation system that drives you around the block again and again.

Great visionaries have a secret weapon against mental comfort. Marshall Goldsmith offers three very strong and practical recommendations on how to outfight comfort.

> *'We're really talking about a scalable vision, not a limited vision. Comfort is the enemy of vision as it keeps you from changing. Many people said to me exactly the same thing if you live too comfortably, you develop a prison.*
>
> *Now in order to achieve what I do as a coach, people need three things.*
>
> *They need courage. You need the courage to look in the mirror. Vision takes courage. And a lack of courage can kill vision.*
>
> *The second thing you need to successfully execute a vision is humility. You need to admit you need to involve other people. You can't do it by yourself. You can kill a vision because of your arrogance.*
>
> *The other one is discipline. Successfully implementing a vision requires day to day discipline. If you don't have discipline then you will not achieve the vision. Discipline is very hard'.*

Exercising Your Inner Excellence

I have an old personal friend whose name I don't want to mention publicly, and so let's call him Ian. Some years ago, he made a brilliant investment in a financial institution and put much of the profit into his own business. A couple of years ago, his very promising project on renewable energy went bust with a few million euros in losses because of poor management and lack of leadership.

Now he works on a new project in the same field in Canada. As he is a close friend, I offered him a helping hand with no strings attached. Ian responded that he needs to solve issues with potential partners and set up technical processes first and then think of something else, like vision and leadership. He is repeating the same mistakes, and I worry it will once again cost him dearly.

If you are not creating a vision for your business, then you will soon prepare a funeral speech for it. In personal life, this is like taking one's talents and desires, and burying them deep.

Being well-intended is only the beginning. Developing yourself and your vision and gaining mastery of it is key. All positive changes come as result of focused preparation. You must exercise your inner excellence every day.

Don't expect positive changes in your life to come from others. Don't expect someone else to be more interested in your success than you are. In fact, others are more likely to impede your vision in the early stages. The work to implement your vision has to come from you. Only then can you hope that others will be inspired by it.

As Raphael Louis said, 'Vision is a beautiful instrument and a gift at the same time. As with any psychological instrument it demands being fully inclusive, psychologically involved and well prepared to manage it masterfully'.

A similar suggestion came from Olga Uskova who leads a global AI project.

'To get prepared you must delete everything excessive that interrupts thinking and acting and make the remaining as simple as possible. This is very hard work, penetrating very deeply into the specifics of what you do. You must know and understand yourself.

This is similar to a cellist who must play-play-play until the sound is perfected to the highest purity and you resonate with it. You must work your fingers to the bone every day. You must improve and improve again to reach mastery. Hard work in preparation is non-negotiable. All the talk that you can envision something while lying on a sofa is for the mental wankers'.

First of all, you must define where to allocate your resources and time. Garry Ridge offered his own time-tested prescription.

'I'm a work in progress. I'm consciously incompetent. I'm always asking myself – 'Why do I believe this to be true? What stories am I telling myself today that I need to clarify?' The thing is that time, talent, and treasures, none of them are abundant. You need to make choices and be deliberate, and you need to make peace with the choices you make. You need to understand that you can't do it all immediately and you have to make peace with that. It's really allocation of resources and the ones that are most scarce are time and talent and treasure. We have to be deliberate with those'.

Courage

Everyone feels fear that penetrates into every cell of the body when standing in front of something huge and yet to be fully explored. Fear is a negative advisor that blocks one's ability to make advanced decisions. Fear is the result of self-doubt and unclear understanding of one's own capacities. This is a normal human reaction. Winston Churchill once said, 'Fear is a reaction. Courage is a decision'. Courage is a skill that helps to overcome fear and can be developed. It depends on how we live every day and get ready to respond to something unusual or seemingly beyond our control. I know this from my experience fishing in rough seas and facing massive gales on a small trawler. At first you feel sick during a moderate storm and scared of not having any control over the situation. Then, gradually you adapt and learn how to manage yourself and what best to do under such rough conditions. At a certain point, you enjoy this tremendous force and almost look forward to it.

Still, courage facing something visible like a storm is one thing while facing something invisible yet extremely powerful is another ball game altogether. As soon as you turn your fear into courage, the logic and experience start providing you with logical answers to the most complicated tasks. It is you who decides whether fear controls you or you ignore it and take control of what you can. David Katz is someone with the courage to challenge a global problem. And win.

'Life is empty and meaningless. It has only the meaning that you give it as it does not come with meaning. This is an original idea to most people because they believe it comes with meaning – that things have purpose.

I think that when you come to a place of life being absolutely abundant, you can choose whatever you want because you see that. When I had the idea for the plastic bank, it was certainly an enormous idea, creating a new monetary system for the world. I recognized that could be a solution for the world to help the poor and never throw money away. Currently, there's almost nine trillion kilos of plastic on Earth, all the plastic ever produced is still here. It' worth roughly $1 per kilo. There's nine trillion dollars of value on the planet and that's only if it's traded once.

The second thought, "David you can't do it. It's too big. You have to go and build a supply chain, a global supply chain. You're going to have to sell to some of the biggest companies in the world. You're going to have a global empire of staff. You're going to have to digitize it and create a platform for the world." Immediately it almost became overwhelming.

And then the ego's attachment to the past appeared and said I'm not the person who could do it. The reason we're even speaking now is because I had a moment of consciousness as the third thought, a gift.

The gift that came to me was this thought – "David, you don't need to be the person who will change the world. You only slowly need to become the person who can.' That was the gift."

While discussing David's experience even further we came to an understanding that visionaries allow their word to determine the world. They are conquering the world by bringing their own meaning to it.

Every long, tough and unknown journey begins with a courageous decision to make it. Vision demands courage as any exploration does. In simple words, courage is the wisest and necessary decision for those who set themselves the task of creating and executing a great vision.

Courage is contagious. The more courage we display in advancing our vision, the more we will inspire others to join us.

Learning

Why discuss learning again? The reason is simple. At the stage when vision is created, visionaries learn even more actively and in a more focused way than before.

Leading requires constant learning. The more responsibility visionaries have, the more they learn. All visionaries are sophisticated learners. They are *learnaholics*. Their minds are already addicted to learning at this stage. Whenever they have a chance to read, observe and meet new people, they use it. They learn about themselves, others, and everything around them.

An old Chinese proverb says: 'Walking ten thousand miles of road is better than reading ten thousand scrolls of books'. This old wisdom is still relevant as no book can replace the experience of meeting new people and seeing different wonders with our own eyes, helping us to understand ourselves and our place in this world.

'Be worldly' – Adam Witty suggests as he uses extensive travel as a form of preparation for reaching new heights in business success, in addition to being a big reader.

'I believe that the people that have the most vision are the worldliest. They are the ones that entertain their minds. They read, they participate in arts and are well-travelled. They are out and about because I believe that vision is partially crafted through your subconscious mind. You need many files in the file cabinet that makes up your subconscious mind to connect dots while you're sleeping; while you're unconsciously thinking about it. And so my view is that people that get out and see the world are able to create great things. It's the richness of all those experiences that actually lead to more effective vision for the future'.

Reading one hundred books a year seems a lot but not for these people. Reading is a must for all of the visionaries I know.

This is their habit. The difference is that at his stage their reading list is much more highly focused.

They observe people thoroughly, which helps them to understand and find common language with people from different backgrounds. They sense people's problems and how to help them find ever better solutions for them.

Inner Excellence

Vision grows along the way, making it difficult to predict how it will be realised. This is a life-long, even a generational journey. Every vision-driven action gets you further from your starting point with no chance for return to that place of comfort, demanding greater psychological strength each day.

When we talk about vision creation and execution, I fully support Brian Tracy's view – 'Aspire greatly; anything less than a commitment to excellence becomes an acceptance of mediocrity'.

Growing inner excellence is primarily a psychological challenge. I turned this question to Prof. Nabhit Kapur, Psy.D., an expert in psychological well-being. Prof. Kapur is a PsychoPreneur, mental health advocate, author, three-time TEDx speaker and globally decorated ambassador of mental health and peace with over 200 recognitions from 30 countries around the world. Prof. Kapur is the founder and president of PeacfulMind Foundation Fellowship programme. He established the global Youth Mental Health Forum, a platform that helps to train youth in psychological first aid. Also, the global initiative, Global Chamber of Business Leaders, was built on his vision of business for peace and wellness.

'When you have a vision obviously, there are two things – one is the skills, which you already have. You can't take those for granted of course. You have to keep on growing and evolving every day because as an entrepreneur or as a leader you know well that things are changing every day.

You can't just sit on what you have with your own skills and just maneuver around them because that would become redundant. You have to keep

on growing and evolving every day. I want to grow and evolve as a person. I want to be holistic in myself.
When you create a vision, you create the possibility that you can achieve your goal at the same time. There are definitely psychological processes involved in it. Number one, even before creating a vision a person has to be psychologically fit'.

Vision demands constant inner preparation to get ready for any challenges and to fight that psychological battle. The fight for vision is not physical.

Nothing is more devastating for a forward-thinking vision than an old and rigid mindset. While growing inner excellence and psychological strength, one is getting closer to tomorrow's goals.

Credibility and Confidence

In one of our conversations, Marshall Goldsmith said to me, 'You need to have credibility, because if you don't have credibility, you're not going to have a vision of magnitude'. By following Marshall's logic, we can say that credibility attracts investments in the form of people's engagement and effort. In turn, credibility is the result of your confidence in what you do.

Asheesh Advani considers confidence enhancement a core attribute of a strong leader.

'Being prepared means growing your confidence. I've had to learn to be a better leader as I've taken on a role that involves leading a very global organization with lots of cultural nuances with teams over 100 countries. When you as leader recognize your own weaknesses, limitations, and learning opportunities, and you are authentic about that with your team, I think they also invest in their own personal development. When they see you devoting time to doing 360 reviews for your own leadership, working with an executive coach, and being transparent about what you want to improve, they feel more confident to do the same and are willing to share that with others just like you have done with them. Confidence is resilient when it comes from authenticity'.

No one can build a future without confidence. Knowing what to do and how to do it, with confidence and competence, is a must for a visionary leader. People evaluate a leader in much the same way they would a survival guide. They want to see professionalism, confidence and credibility. The leader with confidence is worth ten hesitant ones. The credible leader draws others to himself.

Confidence in a way means defeating yourself again and again. It means defeating your fears and anxieties, your tendencies to procrastinate. This is not possible in the long term if you are only doing it for yourself. Good leaders must build themselves for others. Confidence comes when one is sure that he or she fulfils and even surpasses his or her commitments to people.

Knowledge Bank

All the knowledge within your reach must be pulled together, which will help to form a knowledge bank and turn it into an incredible advantage. Alex Goryachev perfectly stated this essential part of preparation, reflecting his experience of working with companies around the world.

> 'When you think about any organization, often their biggest asset is the knowledge of their employees. It's essential that any business creates a safe space to tap into that knowledge. When implemented, this goes a long way towards your best employees and, therefore, your customers, as you are creating an environment where opinions are valued, taken into consideration and can be brought to life through improving operational processes, products or services. Continuous investment in transparent, open culture is essential to create and maintain that environment. The opposite of transparency is so called "silo mentality," which is the mortal enemy of organizational success. If you let silo mentality prevail in your organization, you will encourage low morale, destroy productive culture, reduce efficiency, and obviously kill innovation. If knowledge isn't shared, no true vision and strategy can exist'.

If we consider vision as something huge and alive, then we can only imagine how much knowledge this living giant demands to live and grow successfully. I will phrase this a bit differently – how much knowledge does a child need for every stage of life? A vision needs even more knowledge. Vision's survival and growth depend on knowledge that is immediately accessible, full-bodied and renewable.

The level of knowledge in a team directly correlates with its level of success. This defines how a company is able to find the best solutions, be innovative, or how efficient it is in solving problems. The company's wisdom resides in this bank.

At the same time, vision is created on knowledge, and thus its growth and capitalisation depend on the growth of that knowledge bank. Don't plan your vision without securing a sufficient knowledge bank.

A CLICK Self-assessment Form

I learned one simple rule for personal and professional improvement – learn like a child when starting every new project or facing a new stage of life. Yet, effective development demands well-planned everyday effort and a means of assessing progress. Every gap in preparation is reflected in delays at a later stage.

A weekly CLICK self-assessment form can help to track and monitor your evolution as a visionary. CLICK stands for Courage, Learning, Inner Excellence, Credibility and Confidence, and Knowledge bank.

C for courage

As we already discussed, courage is a skill that can be developed. To develop it, I don't recommend you jump into cold water every day or do something risky. Instead I would ask you to look at it differently. Courage is acting and thinking boldly in the face of something unexplored, huge and complicated. In such cases, one competes not against somebody else but against one's own self and fears.

Ask yourself these five simple questions while developing courage:

- What disrupted your thinking and progression with your vision?
- What was your response to this disruption?
- What is the nature of your fears?
- What fear have you managed to fight or seriously reduce its impact over the last week?
- Did you enjoy something that scared you before?

You can develop courage by asking yourself bold questions and finding answers that lie beyond your own fears and usual habits of thinking. Only by challenging yourself can you become a catalyst for change and thrive as a ground-breaking visionary. Lack of courage leads to a professional and personal crisis.

L for learning

Learning is a prerequisite of personal and professional growth. Please answer these five questions as honestly as possible.

- What gaps in knowledge or areas for improvement have you realised over the last week?
- How many new people have you met and talked to this week?
- What new knowledge or information sparked your curiosity?
- How you will put the knowledge acquired into practice?
- What kept you from learning more?

Only by learning can one develop one's ability to think critically. There are no shortcuts or any valid excuses to avoid learning. You can fake it for a while but one thing you can be sure of is that the future will eventually reveal your weakness.

I for inner excellence

Motivation is meaningless unless you are fully committed to your vision regardless of the challenges you'll face. Every day is about overcoming those challenges and becoming stronger in the process. This requires authenticity, strong self-awareness and adaptability.

There are five questions to answer on a regular basis:

- How well do you know yourself?
- What behavioural change is needed?
- How do you enhance your authenticity?
- What recent challenge or problem drove you off the rails?
- What have you learned about your own potential?

Daily pressures and challenges will threaten to derail you. Staying on task requires focus and discipline. Becoming stronger with every challenge you overcome will strengthen your vision as well, and make you a better version of yourself. In turn, you will inspire others to join you on the journey.

Confidence and credibility

A confident leader doesn't waste his or her energy on self-doubt. Instead, that energy is directed to whatever is necessary to make the vision a reality. A real visionary gains credibility by adding value and delivering on his promises. Ask yourself these five questions:

- What positive and valuable thing have you done for people over the past week?
- What promises are left unfulfilled?
- How much did you learn about yourself?

- What undermined your 'I'?
- Have you given people a reason to follow?

If a leader is not confident, then his people won't be. How much doubt a leader casts on his people is a reflection of a leader's confidence. Let your inner excellence be a magnet for people.

Knowledge bank

Knowledge becomes valuable and practical when shared. Its incredible power is added to by many people. Building up knowledge is best done as part of a team.

Answer these five questions and ask your team to do the same every week.

- What has your team learned over the last week?
- Do you need to recruit a new member because of a lack of knowledge in the team?
- Did all the members contribute to the knowledge bank?
- How much have your team members learned from each other?
- How has your team translated problem-solving tasks into lessons learned?

Encourage your team to contribute to the knowledge bank by sharing knowledge and your journey in acquiring it. Your minimum aim is to eradicate gaps in the level of knowledge among team members. Your main goal is to enhance its peak level amongst the team.

The CLICK self-assessment form will help fight anti-vision you. It will take about an hour or so every week to answer these questions and reflect on them, which will help gauge your progress in building your vision. The stronger you become, the greater the vision you will be able to create and execute.

Conclusion

Vision is a living creature that needs to be nurtured in order to grow. Therefore, visionaries must develop themselves for the growth of their vision.

Master yourself to master your vision. The more capable a leader becomes, the more value he or she will be able to offer to others. Those who have nothing can contribute nothing to the future, or even to themselves.

Practical Tips

- Everyone is the CEO of his own vision and must be prepared accordingly.
- We always have time to correct mistakes if we are courageous enough to admit them and have a strong will to change for the better.
- There is always a good mentor or coach behind every man or woman of success who helps to develop the capacity for achieving exceptional heights. A good mentor or coach helps to attune critical thinking and personal development.
- No one is the smartest person in this world who knows everything about himself and his business. I'm not the smartest either, and someone should tell me the moment I do something stupid. Otherwise, I will be harming others and myself without even realising it, and often in a big way. It is a matter of being coachable or teachable and being humble enough to accept that every new knowledge and skill learned makes you better.
- A new version of vision is often cannibalised by an old mentality and habits. One must strike a balance between drawing lessons from the past and being stuck in it.

- Set yourself up for success by being prepared. Ignoring preparation means setting yourself up for a painful failure. Would you risk your long-created vision because of a lack of preparation? Many do and fail as result. No one builds a stronghold on quicksand.

- Internal motivation springing from a clear vision can help inspire others to find their own motivation. External motivation without self-discovery is an artificial form of encouragement that only reveals those desperately aiming to get into a position of power at any cost.

- Authenticity keeps ego on a short leash.

Part II

Making Vision Strong

4

The Six Criteria
of a Strong Vision

'It is amazing what you can accomplish if you do not care who gets the credit'.

Harry S. Truman

The beauty of vision lies in its structure. That may sound strange but whenever we want to create something strong and beautiful, it must be clearly and effectively structured, whether it be an aeroplane, software or vision. Thus, we talk about engineering vision to make it robust, reliable, flexible, simple and beautifully proportional.

The challenge is that a vision is not a mere statement written so it can be nailed on an office wall and gives people something to look at when waiting for the meeting to start. Signs and statements don't define the future but emphasise an inability to create a vision that is strong, elegant, practically functional and appealing to all. Not to mention that it must be future-ready, shock-resistant and idiot-proof.

I talked over this issue with Martin Lindstrom. Martin is the founder and Chairman of Lindstrom Company, the world's leading brand and culture transformation group, operating across 5 continents and more than 30 countries. *TIME* magazine has named Martin Lindstrom one of the 'World's 100 Most Influential People'. For three years running, Thinkers50, the world's premier ranking resource of business icons, has selected Martin to be among the world's top 50 business thinkers. Martin Lindstrom is a high-profile speaker and author of seven *New York Times* best-selling books, translated into 60 languages. His book *Brand Sense* was critically acclaimed by *The Wall Street Journal* as 'one of the five best marketing books ever published', *Small Data* was praised as 'revolutionary' and *TIME* magazine described his book *Buyology* as 'a breakthrough in branding'.

> *'I've always worked with visions and I think that the understanding of vision has changed over the years. In the old days it was something that companies would hang on a plaque or in a picture frame in the lobby and it really wouldn't have a lot of impact on the organisation. It was a very nice welcoming message. What I realised happened was that if it's a really powerful vision, it really would have a profound impact on the organisation and on its culture.*
>
> *However, a lot of companies still have a huge disconnect between real vision and just having that plaque on the wall in the reception. I have realised over the years that vision has been rebranded now and people treat it more or less like purpose'.*

Vision should be more than a sign. It should provide firm ground on which to stand and a lofty goal to reach for. This requires that it be carefully constructed. A successfully crafted vision will attract and motivate people to make it a reality. As it comes closer to reality, it attracts an ever-growing pool of supporters.

Leadership is blind without vision. Vision defines and explains why and where effort should be focused. The leader therefore has to communicate the vision effectively to inspire others.

The greatness of a vision matters more than the size of the organisation. Great vision allows organisations to grow and remain valuable for many years ahead. It acts as a force multiplier by helping to solve multiple problems for people across countries and continents.

What elements or criteria define the greatness of a vision? Vision must address people's needs, be easy to understand, scalable and growing, lead to success and stir the emotions. Every great vision has six firm criteria that reflect these properties – stimulus, scale, spotlight, scanning, simplicity and excitement.

Stimulus

Stimulus – Vision reflects the highest purpose of leadership – purposeful acting for and with people. Vision should include the actual benefits for those affected by it. This passion for people must include – to differing degrees – employees, customers, leaders themselves, employees' families and society at large.

In personal life, if we don't see our dearest folk benefiting from the future that we envision for them then it is not a vision. If we don't envision our dearest people in the pictures of the future, it has little value for them and in turn little value for us. It must reflect a value created for people involved in the course of our lives.

Vision flourishes if the credit for its development is given to all involved. The main stimulus of vision is people and caring for their needs. In this sense, a visionary becomes a father or mother responsible for making everyone feel comfortable and gaining substantial benefit from being a part of it. Strong vision makes people family members, not strangers.

Garry Ridge has thought long about the nature of vision. He views vision as being an absolute if it brings value to people and makes their involvement enjoyable at the same time.

> 'The most beautiful definition of leadership I've heard is "leadership is not about being in charge, it's about taking care of the people in your charge." I think your definition of stimulus is absolutely correct and I say "yes" to it. We are here to serve others and I think that's certainly very important and there is more and more evidence every day. I love what Aristotle said in 384 BC, – "Pleasure in the job puts perfection in the work." If a leader can bring pleasure to the work of the people that follow the leader then the outcome is going to be more beneficial for people, then it's an absolute'.

Garry Ridge's comment led me to think about the multidimensional nature of stimulus as one of the core criteria. If we assume that vision stands for value and pleasure for people, then surely something else should be involved as well. To grasp deep meaning we must have a three-dimensional view.

This realisation came into focus in a conversation with David Katz.

> 'Stimulus without response is just a stimulus. There is always a space between stimulus and response. People wouldn't respond to something if they don't have it or it is not good for them.
>
> Think of the difference between a man and a deer grazing in the woods. The deer flees immediately when it hears a noise. There's no space in between the stimulus and response in the deer's flight. If we talk about a man, there is a space between the stimulus and response; the man will hear a noise and there will be a space before the response. And the man will have a decision at that moment. It's in the decision that his life lies. The space between the decision and the response is where your life appears to be meaningful. We are products of the space between the stimulus and the response'.

Therefore, a strong vision should cause an immediate or almost immediate response from people to be involved and not to flee. In the Foreword to *Prisoners of Our Thoughts* (2017) written by Alex Pattakos and Elaine Dundon, Stephen Covey wrote, 'Between stimulus and response there is a space. In that space is our power to choose our response. In our response lies our growth and our freedom'. This is the third element of stimulus that I look for.

Stimulus comes in three stages – value for people, their natural response to get involved, and enjoyment from being involved. Initially, a vision is created as a response to people's needs or desires. It demands people's active involvement to make it happen.

Without stimulus, the vision collapses immediately because it is not grounded in people and their desires. It will collapse without being noticed. This is what often happens in many businesses when they shift their attention from people to the bottom line.

Scale

Scale – Vision should be of great breadth and depth with potential for extension at later stages. Vision never leads to or accepts a dead end. It shows multiple potentials for expansion. In other words, good vision is always scalable.

Scaling of vision begins with a visionary who is always a work in progress. As Garry Ridge said about himself – 'my vision statement doesn't have a period at the end'. As a visionary grows, his vision grows too. The vision shrinks as soon as the visionary stops growing. For vision to be long-lasting, flexible and scalable, a visionary must be prepared for change, flexibility and growth.

To be a visionary leader, one needs to see not just beyond conventional restrictions, a thought shared by David Katz.

'We live in an unlimited abundance and infinite Universe. Vision lives as a manifestation of the infinite abundance. I would say that if you have boundaries, then there is no vision. Boundaries come from an ego attachment. It's finite and lives only inside of you'.

A visionary has the ability to grasp an ever-changing world. The size of our ego defines whether we have a broad peripheral vision or one bounded by tunnel vision. Peripheral vision is important and often underappreciated. When we have peripheral vision, we can focus on things we need and find them everywhere.

To be able to scale the vision one should maintain an appropriate cognitive distance from it. This allows us to see the broader picture while keeping the important details in sight. Standing too close only allows one to see the details while losing the whole picture. Standing too far away means losing important details from which the vision is created. In the first case, one loses the whole meaning of the vision for nothing. In the second case, the vision becomes detached from reality.

Scale is not only about breadth but also about depth. This is simply about adding value and exploiting opportunities that come as vision grows. This is about in-depth relationships with customers, in-depth market penetration, in-depth utilisation of potential and offering new products and services.

Amit Kapoor is one of the best to talk about the relations of scale and vision. Prof. Amit Kapoor, PhD, is Honorary Chairman at Institute for Competitiveness, India; President of the India Council on Competitiveness and Editor-in-Chief of *Thinkers*. He is the Chair for the Social Progress Imperative & Shared Value Initiative in India and sits on the Board of Competitiveness Initiatives in Mexico, Netherlands, Italy and France and University of Vermont's SEMBA Advisory Board.

He has been inducted into the Competitiveness Hall of Fame administered by the Institute for Strategy and Competitiveness at Harvard Business School in addition to being the recipient of the Ruth Greene Memorial Award winner for writing the best case of the year, from North American Case Research Association (NACRA).

Amit is also the author of bestsellers *Riding the Tiger*, which he has co-authored with Wilfried Aulber and *The Age of Awakening:*

The Story of the Indian Economy Since Independence published by Penguin Random House.

'An organisation or a person will only be known by the contribution that he actually makes. The contribution that you're actually doing should be scalable. Not necessarily that it has to have scale but the scale could also get defined in many interesting ways for me. As an author, scale would mean how many people are actually looking at my book. It does not really mean that I have to publish hundreds of books. The question is whether I'm able to impact people's lives or not. For me, when I'm doing something with the Government of India, then I'm trying to create an impact for 1.3 billion people living in India each day of my life. Regardless of the work I do, scale comes to a matter of impact'.

Scale is about the ever-growing impact of a vision. If vision doesn't have potential for extension, either in breadth or in depth, then something is wrong. A strong vision relies on an abundance of opportunities.

Spotlight

Vision assumes responsibility, immediate and extended. The greater the vision, then the greater the responsibility for its impact on people's lives and the legacy that will be left afterwards. As Peter Drucker said, 'Leadership is not rank, privileges, title or money. It is responsibility'.

Why spotlight, and what is it? Business success begins with responsibility. The same applies in our personal life where responsibility for others is taken for granted. No great achievement is ever built on blaming others, but rather on taking responsibility for others. Leadership is like being on Broadway for 24 hours a day, 365 days a year, with a spotlight on everything you do.

A visionary leader's duty and responsibility is to help people become the best version of their selves. In this sense, there are good leaders with vision who take this responsibility and a bunch of people who call themselves leaders but never take responsibility.

Vision assumes a whole range of responsibilities. Adam Witty sees responsibility as something taken-for-granted in a range of obligations.

> '*I do believe that vision creates responsibility. And so for leaders that have a vision that isn't seen by others. They have a social, a moral and ethical responsibility to make sure that it is a positive vision that leads to the betterment of people that pursue it. If the result of pursuing that vision is that people are worse off, then that vision should not be pursued*'.

I found that when we talk about vision, one simple term can have a huge difference in drawing people into it. For instance, when we talk about strategic plans, we talk about a 25-year horizon. When we talk about vision and impact on the next generation, we assume the same time range, 25 years. Both sound similar, but it creates a different sense of responsibility. In the first case, such a long range sounds illusive as, by that time, many will either quit their job or retire. In the second case, we immediately think about responsibility towards the next generation, our children.

This led me to think about responsibility and its relation to vision. Marshall Goldsmith responded.

> '*If you have a very limited vision, it comes with limited responsibilities. If you have a larger vision it comes with larger responsibility. In other words, the degree of responsibility depends on the magnitude of the vision*'.

Many wish to do something great and incredible. At the same time, no one should take on something that is out of their control. Those who do the latter can be recognised by being quick to refuse responsibility. Those who are not prepared to take responsibility shouldn't think about leadership.

Think of explorers such as Columbus, Magellan, Amundsen or Elon Musk, Sergey Brin and Bill Gates. They all took responsibility as a mandatory obligation for exploring new terrain. They took huge responsibility that comes with incredible opportunities, the kinds of opportunities only available to pioneers.

Think for a moment – responsibility with opportunity. It may be intimidating to take on all that responsibility, but it will reward you in return. The same can be said about all visionaries involved in the creation of this book.

Scanning

Watch for signs and clues in pursuit of your vision while choosing the best path to success. They will be easy to follow if the vision is strong. A visionary sees the signs on his way to success. If one keeps his mind and eyes open, then those signs are always around in different forms – words of encouragement, expressions of real need from strangers, signals of potential risk and answers to critical questions coming from unexpected perspectives.

Scanning is vital for listening to pain points, spotting trends and seeing where and how value can be added. Visionary leaders see what other people don't see. Their conscious and subconscious mind are always working. Scanning is imprinted into a visionary's daily routine. It becomes second nature, or as Olga Uskova commented,

'When you do something or build something, you catch and fix your eyes on things like – here is painful, here is very good, here is tough, there is something else. You read signs all the time, restlessly, consciously and unconsciously'.

The pace of change is only increasing. Think about the simple fact that while you read the previous few lines of this book, a number of changes happened in different parts of the world – a brilliant idea that may change the way we treat cancer was born, a serious market change occurred and we will see it on tomorrow's trades and many other things. Somewhere a butterfly has spread its wings with effects no one can predict, and scanning this moment is critical.

Having known Marshall Goldsmith for a while, I'm aware of how well he reads different changes and why he pays so much attention to them.

> 'The world is changing so rapidly. There are two different issues when we talk about vision – a vision itself and a second issue is its execution. A vision without execution is only an idea, it's meaningless. What you're talking about is in order to have execution. We live in a rapidly changing world. We have very little stability. The pace of change is only going up. The pace of change we experience today is the slowest pace of change we will ever experience for the rest of our lives. It's not going to slow down'.

Scanning is essential. If you ignore scanning, then your vision is at risk. If we think about the Industrial Revolution or the Digital Revolution, most businesses were wiped out because they didn't pay attention to new market trends. They denied what was going on around them. We have to pay attention to the world around us, pick up on subtle cues and adjust our vision accordingly.

Many leaders have suffered because they failed to see a change coming. The simplest example is Nokia, a former leader in mobile phones that lost the game because of a refusal to scan the changing environment and market.

I asked Stuart Crainer about the importance of scanning. Stuart is a co-founder of Thinkers50, the first-ever global ranking of management thinkers, dubbed 'the Oscars of Management Thinking' by the *Financial Time*. Since 2001, the scope of Thinkers50 has broadened to include a range of activities that support the mission of providing innovative access to powerful business and management ideas – ideas that will make the world a better place.

Stuart is also the former editor of London Business School's award-winning magazine *Business Strategy Review*. His book credits include *The Management Century* and a biography of the management guru Tom Peters. He has taught in the international MBA programme at IE Business School and in executive education programmes around the world, including the strategic leadership programme at Oxford University. Stuart is a Visiting Professor at Warwick Business School. He is also the author of *Atlantic Crossing*, based on his experiences sailing the Atlantic.

> '*Scanning is vital. Today, it is very hard for many leaders to do it because their short-sightedness isolates them from the context of reality. Once you become a leader to get accurate information and for people to tell you the truth is not easy while staying aligned with that reality is critical*'.

Keeping up with change demands a great deal of emotional intelligence, education and experience. Education is when you read the fine print, experience when you don't. At the same time, education and experience allow us to generate learning capacity and intuition. By the way, intuition is taken as the highest form of intelligence.

A strong vision is usually associated with believers with strong imagination. Why? They are excellent at spotting tiny signs of unusual opportunities. Attention to these signs and clues helps visionary leaders to craft the most effective path to success.

Simplicity

Vision is elegant thinking about complicated things. A great vision is genuinely easy to understand and never complicated. A vision is not a vision unless it's understood. Simplicity lets people believe in vision. If the vision is complicated most people will ignore it. Therefore, even a vision's physical form must be simple. Vision operates and makes execution possible from its simplicity.

The simpler the vision in its core meaning, the easier it can be shared with employees, customers and partners and thus, easier to scale inside and outside an organisation. Simplicity of vision allows it to be shared easily with and between employees, from employees to customers and among customers.

Complication is the enemy of great vision. If things are too complicated and too difficult to grasp, then most likely this is not a real vision but an overcomplicated puzzle. No one can solve complex problems for people without attracting supporters and developing empathy on a big scale if the vision is too complicated. Too much complexity simply turns people off.

Simple is always better, yet simple is harder than complex. There is a famous phrase of Oscar Wilde – 'I would have written you a short letter, but I only had time to write you a long one'. When communicated, a vision must be understood by any ordinary person. If an ordinary person doesn't understand your vision, then you don't have one.

If people can't understand it easily, then they can't pursue it or achieve it. If you can explain it to a 10-year-old with a handful of words and they understand, then your vision is simple enough.

Amit Kapoor uses a 'KISS' approach to evaluate ideas in terms of simplicity.

'I think one of the most important things is there's a very simple principle called "KISS" – Keep It Simple Stupid. If I'm able to keep things simple that is when they actually begin to be effective. If you're going to complicate it then it may look exotic but at the end of the day, it is not really going to take you anywhere at all. If you can explain it in simple words, then you have a really powerful idea'.

Simplicity is very important, but it's really difficult to do. Not many people have the gift of presenting a vision in simple and accessible language. The simpler the vision, the easier it is for people to understand and to rally around it.

Again, Marshall Goldsmith's wisdom is shown in predicting the growing importance of simplicity.

'I'm a great believer in simple things. If it's not simple, people don't remember it. In the new world people's attention span is not going up, but down. You have to be able to communicate these simple ideas'.

Simplicity connects vision with people. It allows all involved to stay on the same path – even when they come from different approaches – and thus contribute to the accomplishment of the vision.

Excitement and Passion

Vision provokes strong emotions. A strong vision is always accompanied by excitement and passion.

Excitement equals passion that gives an emotional power to a vision. A strong vision brings strong excitement that is difficult to contain. Strong excitement and passion are highly contagious. A simple and compelling vision excites more passion than any mere goal.

John Spence sees excitement and passion as emotional drivers of vision.

'A strong vision brings excitement. At the same time, I know visionaries who don't jump up and down and give rousing speeches to motivate their people. They don't show a lot of emotion but under their calm exterior there is a raging fire. They are so laser-focused and they are so passionate that you can physically sense it. They're going to achieve what they said they were going to achieve. The obvious depth of their personal commitment to the vision is deeply inspiring to their people'.

You can be a very humble, quiet and not excitable leader, but everyone can see your deep burning passion. A visionary can't hide the emotions arising from that vision, and they spill out anyway.

The fact is that your vision is bigger than you. I know from experience, these strong emotions have woken me up in the middle of the night, driving me to write something down or make me desperate to find someone to talk to about my vision.

Actually, passion is serious business itself. Sania Ansari sees passion being critical to achieving something great and being happy at the same time – 'you cannot achieve something great unless you want it with all your heart, unless you're very passionate about it and it makes you happy'.

A compelling vision can't be realised without being emotionally supported. These emotions drive people to put themselves through anything uncomfortable and challenging in executing a vision.

Stronger Together or 5S&EP Model

The six criteria of a strong vision are interlinked, interdependent and overlapping. Each of them is indispensable. Take just one element of the construct and the whole vision will fall apart. In other words, the golden ratio wouldn't be there.

The structure of vision can be visualised by using the 5S&EP model presented in Figure 4.1

The beauty of vision that attracts people is in the harmony of these six elements. Vision doesn't tolerate weak elements as it destroys its balanced beauty.

Are all six criteria of your vision in harmony? If not, check what criterion or criteria demand improvement again and again until your vision becomes harmonious, appealing, functional and future-focused.

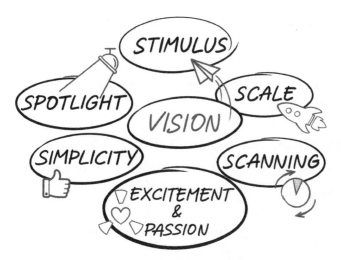

Figure 4.1   Six Criteria of Vision (5S&EP).

Vision Viability Test

Vision must be revised on a monthly basis to verify its relevance, viability, functionality and growth potential. A Vision Viability Test offers the simplest and most practical way of evaluating a vision.

These eighteen questions will help you and your team to maintain the viability of a vision at every stage of its development.

Stimulus: You don't raise children for yourself, you give yourself to raise them. Similarly, you create vision not for yourself, but to live for people.

- Who will benefit from your vision?
- How does it answer people's deep desires?
- Why should people respond to your vision?

Scale: A vision that doesn't grow would die suddenly.

- How much can you expand your vision? (geography, population)
- What further changes may the vision trigger?

- What will the status of your vision be in 5 years? 10 years? 20 years?

Spotlight: If I really care for somebody or something, I feel responsible for what I do.

- Whose skin is in the game, yours or that of others?
- Who shares responsibility for the consequences of a vision?
- How do you understand your responsibility?

Scanning: Vision is the ability to see something that others don't see and turn it into a result.

- How is your vision relevant to the present?
- Will the core of your vision be still relevant, appealing and advanced in five years?
- What's happened in the world over the course of the last month that could affect or enhance your vision?

Simplicity: Professionals tend to present complex ideas in simple words. Pretenders tend to use technical language to justify themselves, not ideas.

- Can you present your vision to professionals in two minutes or less?
- Can you explain your vision to a 10-year-old in two minutes?
- Can your colleagues or supporters explain your vision to their children and get them excited?

Excitement: Your vision is strong and compelling if you see a reflection of your passion in others.

- If you need to express your emotions about vision in two to three words, what would they be?
- Does your vision make people excited?
- Do you spread excitement and passion around you?

Check your vision against this questionnaire once every month as a routine. Keep records of your progress.

Practical Tips

- Poor understanding of a vision's criteria leads to a mess in execution. These criteria are like musical notes in a beautiful song, where without them it sounds like a cacophony. The noise is there but no one is willing to listen it.
- The golden ratio of your vision is defined by people and your job is to help them see it.
- The vision must be simple.
- Vision is beautiful and appealing as long as it's functional and executable. Otherwise, it's just another idea.
- Visionary leadership puts the needs of others above all. Today it is a competitive advantage for a few – tomorrow it will be the norm for all.
- Vision is accompanied by strong confidence in achieving the goal and adding value to many people. This brings happiness that is difficult to contain, one that is infectious.
- Vision is a gift that must be multiplied. The ability to multiply that gift depends on the leader's ability to influence. The greater the vision, the greater the demand for strong and far-reaching influence. This helps to scale a vision in a big way.

5

Communication: The Seventh Element of a Compelling Vision

'The important thing in communication is understanding what isn't said'.

Peter Drucker

Communication makes vision visible and attractive to others. It can inspire the visionary's passion in others or drive people away. A poorly communicated vision is dead if not successfully shared with others.

Communication is the seventh critical element of a compelling vision. This is an essential property of vision whose primary role is to make vision a collective property, giving it away so others can participate in it. A vision's strength is determined by how well it is communicated to others. When this is done well, it can generate any number of unexpected results.

In practical terms, attracting investors is critical. Attracting as many supporters as possible is even more critical and far more difficult. Only by communicating as broadly and actively as possible does vision gain its full viability and functionality.

Language

Vision often requires using old terms in new ways or even inventing new terms. This makes communication even more critical as the visionary is in some ways trying to communicate not just a new idea but new elements of language as well.

Language defines areas of human activity. Approximately 1,000 neologisms are added to the English language each year. All these new words appear as a result of exploring new areas of life while fleshing out a vision. Some words come, some go. Today, we are 'Googling' for information because of Google, not searching as we did a decade ago. At the same time, young generations are hardly aware of the term 'apartheid', which almost disappeared because of Nelson Mandela's vision.

Another good example of a strong merging of language and vision is Apple. Apple is a creator of change on a global scale, yet its language is very simple and human. This is best reflected in their products that are renowned for their simplicity and ease of understanding with regard to navigation. Whatever the technology they invented over the years, whether the Rubber Band technology or iPad technology, when you hit a button or touch a screen, we can see how their vision has affected their product development. A brief glance at their sales figures reveals how effective this approach has been.

A new term that applies to inventions is 'disruption'. I don't think the inventors of gun powder were thinking of disruption, yet it is an accurate description of its effect. We coined the term disruption to highlight a new understanding of inventions as things that can dramatically affect not just their immediate market but the world at large.

Language defines the art of transmitting and reading signals between people. Language defines communication as a vehicle of transmitting messages and stories between people without losing the quality of human emotions and perspectives. It defines the use of acceptable and forbidden metaphors. Language describes values and allows them to be communicated to all corners of the world.

Visionaries use language as an instrument to connect minds and hearts. The effect of their vision, whether it succeeds and changes the world or is passed over is largely the result of the visionary's ability to use language.

Raphael Louis emphasised the role of language:

> 'Most important is to develop a language to communicate your vision, a language that fully expresses your vision so everyone will understand you. It is a thin line between being able to spread your vision or not. Clear and simple language allows me to position myself as a visionary and leader'.

A visionary is a creator of new ideas that become common for millions of people. At the same time, we must consider that people often relate to the same things differently. Even a term as common as 'common sense', often needs clarification. The visionary's duty is to ensure that his ideas are easily understood by more than just a select few.

Vision is a well-structured thought that becomes words that are turned into actions. There is an old adage 'do not preach in a language no one can understand'. The language of vision should connect different understandings into a common and clear one. This should be a language of common values, the language that enables people to create a future together.

Alex Goryachev sees language as responsible for creating a resonance of action:

> 'When it comes to vision words are as important as actions. They should resonate in people's minds as being both inspirational and pragmatic'.

Language of vision should help to expand the boundaries of our understanding of the world and our role in it as creators while allowing us to celebrate the role of everyone involved in a very prominent way.

In other words, a proper language of vision is a language of love, empathy and care for people's future. Every chapter in this book draws attention to people's needs using the words of love, care, effort, desires and solutions to different problems and issues. Language must be simple, appealing, opening the mind and heart.

Communicating and Sharing

On one of my trips to San Diego, California, I walked into the National Geographic Fine Art Galleries La Jolla at La Jolla village. This is a place where world-renowned and famous photographs from *National Geographic*'s pages are exhibited in large formats, allowing people to see every tiny detail and emotion of those captured moments. These incredible and breathtaking images of people and nature are very touching.

The idea behind the gallery is when you bring a *National Geographic* photograph into your home, you become part of the *National Geographic* legacy. All proceeds from the gallery go to supporting photographers and nature conservation projects.

There is an amazing story behind every one of these iconic images. Walking me through the gallery, Julie, a gallery manager, was excellent at helping me quickly understand each one. Julie wasn't merely communicating but sharing the vision of the project and how the idea of *National Geographic* 'helping people better understand the world and their role in it' is elaborated there. She was so passionate that it immediately touched middle of the vision of connecting the photographers' passion with the souls of visitors.

A couple of days later I discussed the nuances of communicating vision with Stuart Crainer, who is one of the top global experts in communicating vision.

'Communication is essential. You can have a great vision but not tell anybody about it. Then it wouldn't go anywhere far. The best leaders are great communicators and they're quite happy to communicate the same thing in exactly the same way day in day out and I think it must be really

boring at times but that's what the best leaders do. I think you can't tell people what the vision is exactly. They've got to be engaged. You've got to engage with them so that they feel it's a vision that's been shared and they've got a part to play in it.

The biggest problem history suggests is communication. I think corporate history is littered with companies who had brilliant strategies and brilliant ideas and brilliant visions, but didn't have leaders who could communicate them well. I think communication is probably the most important key to making anything happen in any organization.

If you've got a bold and ambitious vision, the onus is on the leader to communicate it. The best leaders are the best communicators.

Listening to other people's take on the vision is probably quite difficult. Their interests and interpretation of it might not quite accord with your interpretation, but I think that takes a lot of work and a lot of patience from a leader'.

Effective communication of vision begins with humility. To communicate a vision effectively a visionary must first stop thinking of himself as a big boss. A visionary is not a king or dictator but an inspirer and doer. Acting superior to others will not gain their support and engagement. To accept feedback, you have to allow yourself to care about their response. Unfortunately, many find this kind of humility very difficult.

Talk simply as one person to another. To keep yourself grounded, do simple work. Wash the dishes, work in the garden, anything to keep yourself from feeling like you are above regular concerns.

Why is communication so critical for success? I asked this of Thomas Kolditz. Thomas is a highly experienced global leader with more than 35 years in leadership roles on four continents. He is Executive Director, Doerr Institute for New Leaders at Rice University, Brigadier General (Retired). General Kolditz is a visionary in the field of leadership training and development. He is the founding Director of the Ann and John Doerr Institute for New Leaders at Rice University – the most comprehensive, evidence-based, university-wide leader development programme in the world. The Doerr Institute was recognised in 2019 as the top university leader development programme by the Association of Leadership Educators.

A retired Brigadier General, Thomas Kolditz, PhD, led the Department of Behavioral Sciences and Leadership at West Point for 12 years. In that role, he was responsible for West Point's teaching, research and outreach activities in management, leader development science, psychology and sociology, and was titled Professor Emeritus after retirement.

Thomas commented in his typical straight-forward style:

'If the vision isn't shared and if people can't see the same thing that the leader is describing then how can they possibly work towards it and how can they possibly take initiative? Maybe they can just plod their way through some lockstep plan. But in order for them to take any initiative they have to be able to see. You know where the leader is headed, where the organization is headed and they really have to buy into it. If the vision is either abstract or so extraordinary that people think it's impossible then it can't happen. Then the organization is going to be very weak and it's going to be pretty unlikely that its goals will be achieved. They'll be unable to get to the vision so part of the leaders' role is to take their confidence and give it to other people in the organization to make other people in the organization believe that it's possible to accomplish that goal'.

Thinking about Thomas's comment I came to a simple thought – visionaries communicate the future. There is not much for us in the past, except for lessons. All our hopes and desires are in the future and this is what we communicate. Thus, communicate for the future you want to create, not the past you aim to leave far behind.

Communication should reflect progress as the vision grows. Supporters must see the results of their effort. Every great success is built on effective communication and its influence determined by how widely it is shared. Poor communication wouldn't allow vision to travel far. Strong and effective communication allows vision to travel across continents and gains supporters everywhere and every day.

Listening

We have heard a million times that all great leaders are great communicators. They intuitively grasp that the viability and success of their vision strongly depends on the effectiveness of their communication. What is often missing is that all great leaders are great listeners. They listen with full attention before they talk. If visionaries have a secret weapon, it is their ability to listen.

Listening is a vital component of communication. In listening to people's problems or receiving feedback, you can find the answers you need if you listen carefully.

Feedback is valuable for those who know where they are going and every suggestion that keeps them on track is invaluable. One gains inspiration, encouragement and confirmation that one is on the right track, whether things are right or wrong, and inspiration for new ideas occurs by listening to others. Being a visionary means serving people, which begins with listening, otherwise, how would you know what they need?

Talkers don't want to hear any feedback from employees or customers because where they want to be is unclear even to them. Talkers only care about their own goals.

Communicating

Communication starts with your immediate team. Your team is your most loyal and immediate supporters and executors of vision. They are co-creators of the vision and will be more effective the more they understand and have a stake in that vision.

I had a long conversation with Amit Kapoor about how he engages his team and communicates vision to every member, particularly new ones.

'I start with the team itself because they are my immediate stakeholders who are actually creating something together. We are all creating it together. I think they need to know or understand what we are really trying to do because they have to be part of the dream itself. If they are not part of the dream they will leave. Very quickly that becomes a very transitory population and not a solid team. It becomes exceedingly important to really explain vision to them in a very subtle and very simple way and they have to buy into that dream because if they do it then they become part of it and they stay with you for a long time.

Having said that I think there is always this thing within the organizations where I feel that it takes some time for people to really see the dream in action. There is always going to be that unique moment of madness of how organizations will think about vision and how they implement it. In practice, the first three to five months would be very tricky for any employee or any person who is new to the team because that's when he's just trying to understand and get a feel for what is really happening. If he or she crosses that short five-month barrier – maybe what you would call the valley of disenchantment – then it just speaks for itself. He can really see his impact and can say – "I'm creating some impact. I'm doing something exciting and doing something interesting".

From a visionary standpoint, the question is whether you want to stay true to it. That is where we're going. Vision has to be effectively communicated at all levels. It has to be engaged with all stakeholders where everybody has to be engaged in it and they need to understand or buy into it. If they don't buy into it that means your communication has no effect'.

Engage the team around your vision. This is a critical function of visionary leaders. Hence, a leader who doesn't care to communicate vision and engage his team is left with a team incapable of making decisions and executing the vision. In other words, don't communicate vision you will confuse your team and make them feel neglected and disposable. A good practice is to ask team members whether they know where the organisation is going or not.

People curse things unfamiliar to them or that they don't understand. Communicate your vision and ideas clearly and as many times as needed. A leader who can't or won't communicate his ideas will be left alone.

How can we engage people in exploring new dimensions and facets of vision or finding solutions to complex problems? Talk to people in a qualitative way. Place a vision or a subject of discussion into the centre of conversation and encourage people to contribute to it. Such an approach makes everyone equal in the interaction and all those involved become contributors to the vision. At the same time, this allows a depth of communication, leading to understanding the real thoughts of the team members instead of encouraging them to just smile submissively.

Quality of communication defines engagement. Alex Goryachev expressed his approach to quality communication in a very practical manner:

> 'We must communicate our vision to our stakeholders and get them onboard. Our employees must understand the value they are creating and be able to communicate it back clearly. A great example of that occurred in 1962 when President John F. Kennedy asked a janitor at NASA – "what do you do?" – "I am here to put a man on the Moon." It is a very strong statement and he understood that his job mattered. When employees understand what the company vision is the culture changes, as it enables people to become more engaged and as a result more focused and empowered. Sadly, I must say that these days a majority of employees do not know what their company is doing and this is a problem'.

Vision becomes real and important for people only when they know about it. A vision needs a strong and clear voice. It must be communicated in such a manner that even nay-sayers would sign up to it. Only then does vision reach its full scale of influence.

Uber provides an excellent example of this. No one even thought about a need for such a modern taxi service. Successful communication at the initial stage of development paved their road to global expansion.

In turn, messy communication equals misunderstanding and massive disengagement. The vision quickly dies.

In all cases, you communicate in simple terms the value the vision brings to people's lives. Often this issue is not considered, as leaders think that employees and customers are disposable. They think that so long as they are making money, then everything is fine.

Such leaders operate on a paradigm that is actually anti-vision. Their anti-vision principles are simple:

- Ignore people and don't bother to think and talk about the benefit to them. People should consume what is offered.
- Keep selling empty promises and misleading information.
- Use unclear and technical language. If others don't understand, that's their problem.

- Don't bother to listen to people as only you know what people need. Thus, you will save time and avoid the risk of altering your plans. In the end, this is your dream, not theirs.
- Timely communication is for those who can't wait.
- Keep communication as inconsistent as possible. Confused people are easier to manipulate.

Sharing Vision

While exploring communication as the seventh element of vision I felt that something was missing. Something that was just beyond my grasp. Here I realised that I must return to the initial question – what is the difference between communicating and sharing vision?

I needed well-tested responses to this question to grasp the difference. I knew that if I called John Spence while he was having his morning cup of ice tea, I had a good chance to hear a deep reflection of John's experience. I called John and galloped straight into this question leaving no chance for him to prepare. John responded with a very interesting comment:

'No matter what organization, one of the biggest challenges is communicating a vivid and compelling vision and strategy for growth. Communicating to me, as far as structure goes, is internal to external. We're communicating it to our stakeholders by sending a consistent message from within our organization.

What is the difference between communicating and sharing? Sharing is very similar to communicating, but sharing has more emotion to it.

We're telling stories and we're giving examples and we're putting more of our personality into it while communicating is more like simply pushing it out. Sharing is all of us together talking about exploring a vision and seeing what it means for all of us emotionally.

Sharing the vision helps people answer the question of why is this so important and why am I personally committed to it? I think that shared vision is something that creates a lot of momentum and motivation inside and outside the organization. Sharing allows a company to motivate employees by giving them an opportunity to be involved in crafting the vision not just being told what it is'.

Compelling vision demands compelling communication where word of mouth is simply not enough. It must be passionately shared to reach hearts. Thus, communication is the core that keeps conversation going and sharing has an in-depth effect in engaging people and turning them into real participants. We communicate information, where a story of success and positive change is shared.

While we need both, sharing comes from the heart and soul and every person is invited to add their own positive thoughts and energy to it. Shared vision is a shared passion, shared emotions, shared engagement and mutual affection. The more you share, the more energy a vision will gain from supporters.

For a vision to succeed, it must be shared in a way that allows people to see things as a visionary does. Sharing vision is a process of transferring the rights of possession – and obligations to execute – them from the visionary to his supporters. At the same time, the role of sharing is to make everyone involved feel equally important regardless of their role. Vision is for all, not for a visionary only.

In practice, visionaries realise they don't have all the answers. They realise that they will need help to solve unforeseen problems along the way. The feedback of supporters is essential to tweaking the vision.

Sharing vision is literally giving away your heart, passion and desires in return for people's sincere engagement, effort and support. This kind of openness generates a deeper commitment from others. This commitment feeds the vision and helps it grow.

What does successful sharing mean? Martin Lindstrom came up with excellent insight and reasons why LEGO has managed to spread its vision to almost every house across the globe:

'When Godtfred Kirk Christiansen, president and CEO of LEGO Group and the LEGO founder's son established the base vision they had back in the day he was well known for calling around to random employees within

the organization at two in the morning and asking them to recite what the brand vision was for Lego. That was based on the notion that if people can't do it in their sleep they can't do it when they're not asleep'.

In this sense, sharing helps get the vision into the unconscious mind.

Fear to Share Leads Nowhere

I've made an interesting observation over the years. A lot of people, particularly young entrepreneurs and start-up enthusiasts, are afraid to share their vision assuming that it will be stolen. Sometimes, they are afraid to the extent of phobia. I saw such cases many times. Even when start-ups come for advice, they are often squeezing words out trying to keep from sharing as much of the vision as possible. The idea can be brilliant, but it will die from lack of communication.

Often the dialogue goes like this – 'Who will support you and your endeavour?' 'We rely on word of mouth'. 'Then, why would people support you if you are hesitant to share something that you have created for them?'

The more information you share, the more people can help you. If you hold something back, then no one can give you ideas or help with information and suggestions or simply help you fix problems. Vision is about transparency and confidence in people's support.

A Practical Magic

Shared vision is critical for encouraging vision ownership by as many people as possible. The sense of belonging or ownership grows from within to bring everyone from outside back inside. Thus, it creates a circle of supporters that grows bigger and bigger with every sharing. It engages shareholders, employees, customers and enthusiasts from all over the world.

We can trace the beginning of communicating a vision to the first words said to a friend, or a message on WhatsApp sent to a colleague. We can't trace its end as it never stops. If a visionary and his team stop communicating, the vision then dies very quickly.

The true magic in communicating vision lies in the ability to encourage ownership of the vision in others. The ownership of vision can be defined by realising who owns the results of the vision. To find the answer ask people one question – do you feel pride when the company or a co-worker experiences success in implementing the vision, or only when you do?

That magic allows one to create a broad network of ambassadors for the vision. Ambassadors help strengthen and spread the vision across continents. This can't be achieved without real interaction whether directly or through those ambassadors. They seed the vision in the minds of people around them. They help increase the boundaries of influence from local to global.

A successful vision inspires a sense of gratitude between the visionary and those who benefit. Gratitude reflects satisfaction with the vision's results. Customers demonstrate this gratitude when they share their positive experience and provide valuable feedback. Customers' positive responses reflect how the vision is grounded in their real needs. Think of Tesla's satisfied drivers who enthusiastically help to convey the company's message.

Well-communicated vision inspires people to see the world in a better light and launches their imaginations beyond existing reality, stimulating more creative input from people involved. Inspiration beats motivation in the long run. It is contagious. It helps lift people towards their higher purpose encouraging us to think beyond the possible.

Consistent communication keeps people engaged, informed and focused on developing the vision. Also, as water crushes rocks little by little, consistent communication crushes scepticism and resistance to change.

Practical Tips

- Communication gives legs to a vision, sharing provides a human touch making communication heartfelt, and language secures common understanding.
- Vision is a never-ending narrative that should thrill people at every stage. Keep the engaging rhythm and consistent pace of telling this life-changing story, making people desire to make their own mark within it.
- The core part of the vision's message is – 'I care for you and stand by you. I'm willing to take risks so you don't have to'.
- Don't be afraid of sharing your vision. It multiplies enormously only by active sharing.
- There is no such thing as remote stakeholders but only poor communication and reluctance to fully share the vision. The best practice is to make everyone an ambassador of the vision.
- Effective communication adds flexibility and strength to the vision while compensating for weaknesses in any of the other six core criteria of vision.
- Vision must be properly communicated and widely shared. It adds momentum even in crisis times when every support and input is needed.
- Consistent and compelling communication guarantees a vision's success. Lack of consistency in communication guarantees failure.
- No force is stronger than people united by a common vision; making decisions together and acting as one. Instilling a shared vision is a goal that precedes profit and is critical for the success of any organisation.

Part III

Execution

6

Aligning Execution with Vision

'To believe in something and not live it is dishonest'.

Mahatma Gandhi

The saddest fact about business reality is that not many visions survive because of poor execution. Unsuccessful execution of vision is such a norm that we don't even pay attention to such stories, taking them as something obvious and routinely expected.

As Marshall Goldsmith says, 'in fact, ideas are like insects. Many are born but few survive very long. The problem is not the idea. The problem is the execution of the idea and what can kill the idea is almost anything'. In this sense, if a vision is a wonder, then successfully executed vision becomes a legend that we all share between us, and talk about it from stages at local and international summits and conferences.

Actually, everyone talks about what good execution looks like and are ready to talk for hours about it. I've heard a million of those stories. The problem is, they didn't lead anyone to success. In fact, people bragging about knowing the shortcuts to success often don't grasp core traits of successful execution or maybe purposely skip this, not knowing the truth.

Most often leaders of all sorts manipulate vision for quick gain and lose sight of that big goal. Noel Ferguson shared his story:

> *'Tomorrow is built today, but it is not clear to all. They pretend. I was on assignment at a large global company, and tasked with helping them implement a five-year plan for a new product/service. The difficulty was, as I reviewed their existing plans to reach the five-year vision, it was clear to me that it was built on straw. I unearthed evidence that the business case had been manipulated, assumptions artificially inflated and stakeholder concerns dismissed.*
>
> *Those who had compiled the business case, had also left the company. The senior team, now frustrated at the perceived lack of progress towards, and deviation from the plan, started kicking people when targets weren't achieved to the level of witch-hunting.*
>
> *The reason is simple – they focused on immediate unrealistic targets instead of focusing on vision and long-term goals as stages of achieving that vision. Therefore, they were pretenders without actual vision.*
>
> *Many people confuse goals for vision. The vision is your desired future state. Goals are the steps you take to reach your vision'.*

Don't worry if you have a similar experience, you are not alone. All have been victims of poor execution. We know how to fail but must learn how to win by executing our visions effectively.

The true test of a vision is in its execution. The code of the future can be cracked only by strong leaders. Visionaries are leaders who managed to turn their vision into reality despite many challenges. None of them talk about sales, operations, or any other functions that ordinary leaders tend to lean on and consider as the core drivers of execution. They talk about strong leadership first.

Strong Leadership

The future complies only with leaders strong enough to manage it. Strong visionary leaders create a vision and guide it to success. The question is – where are these strong leaders?

Martin Lindstrom gets straight to the point with his view:

> *'We have a problem because you have to remember that we live in a world now where consensus increasingly has become very important for everyone to secure. The biggest problem is that vision cannot be created through consensus. It can only be created by strong leadership in my opinion and that's where strong leaders stand out.*
>
> *We are short of the leaders that really see new grounds and people really prepared to follow them. That's the reason why we have a very few visions'.*

Consensus comes into play when a leader has no idea where to go and seeks instead to please everyone. Pleasers don't create value either for others or themselves. They never change anything for good, instead doing harm by never changing anything. Pleasers don't take risks, which is a huge risk itself. They hide their lack of leadership qualities and excessive indecisiveness behind the consensus. Vision demands action. Strong leaders are doers who make vision a reality, pleasers don't.

Another problem with leadership is the tendency to focus on managing bottom lines. Investors and supporters are attracted by promises of a prosperous future and fooled by optimistic quarterly and annual reports that have little in common with five- or ten-year plans or the successful execution of a vision. While the market is interested in the long-term progression, the meaningless KPIs and bottom-line figures are tattooed inside of a lot of leaders' eyelids to make the achievement of the vision virtually impossible.

Such leaders control people to death instead of empowering them. They enthusiastically vote for a vision, where in fact they are sabotaging the greater goal by short-termism and policing processes. Such leaders don't realise that visionary leadership is about empowering people and not about control or micromanagement. Strong leadership is about guiding people.

Control is an illusion. Realistically, most things are out of our control. Nothing in life or business is under our full control. Trying to control too much actually impairs vision.

Excessive control reflects a leaders' lack of self-confidence. They don't trust people to do the job they've been hired for. As a result, weak leaders surround themselves with those who bring them only good news and always say 'yes' to everything.

Such micromanagement reflects micro vision or no vision at all. Instead of tracking alignment of execution and vision, weak leaders cut it short and destroy it well before it can grow. They don't grasp the full picture regardless of their statements. We can see this in all businesses, whether small companies or global corporations.

Another category of dangerous leaders is those driven by their personal ambitions. They will drive everything off a cliff in a chase for their personal satisfaction. You have no doubt met such leaders in the course of your life and career. They don't build anything long term and nothing for others.

What do strong leaders do? Strong leaders connect people, help people grow, guide them, coach them for long-term achievements and restlessly enhances core values. Such a leader assumes responsibility for positive massive transformation that helps people get out of their bubbles and conquer new terrain. This is why a strong leader takes the helm. The strong leader's aim is to achieve success not just for himself, but for all.

In short, strong leaders focus on people, not on themselves. They are purpose-driven, not report worms. They anticipate the future by executing it, not by talking about it.

Culture

If vision is a belief in the positive future, then culture is the belief system that underlies it. Martin Lindstrom sees culture as a roadblock to successful execution if not maintained in a strong and dynamic way:

> *'One of the most critical roadblocks is culture. We're messing about it mainly because leaders think that this is the duty of the marketing*

department, or of the communication department, or whatever. Leaders do not really think about this and that's where you hit a roadblock. That's a serious challenge and that's the reason why a lot of visions quite often fail unless their champions have a very bold and strong leadership ability.

Every single company on planet Earth today is evolving because of technology. It actually made me think that their vision has evolved and now is not what it once was. I think the most well-known and iconic example would be Nokia, it's not that relevant today, but still makes my point. Nokia being a tire company in the old days and becoming a smartphone company meant their original vision ended.

We have multiple generations in a company, each of them representing different forms of culture and if you take your newly born vision and squeeze it on top of them, I'm pretty sure that some people will love it, some people will be fine with it and some people absolutely hate it because they can't find themselves in it. That's where the whole thing breaks down because it does become just a plaque in the lobby and nothing more and it completely falls apart through the different touch points. That is where it has to be embedded into the culture.

A vision at the end of the day is not going to be a graphic identity. It actually has to start with the culture and in my opinion, you really need to take people on a cultural transformation first'.

There are three essential factors about culture that must be considered – culture as the energy behind the success, the role of leaders, and care for people and their growth.

Culture provides the inner psychological energy to an organisation and instils a sense of purpose. Culture is that energy that comes from the joint efforts and enthusiastic fulfilment of duties of all employees, and, as a result, adds spark and life to all processes. If the culture is positive and stimulating, we can expect the desired reaction that results in a superior product and secures growth.

The roots of cultural energy lie deep in the beliefs, desires, concerns and inner reflections of every employee. The combined energy of people who are gathered in the name of achieving the same goals is a tremendous force. Combined together it can defeat any obstacle.

Culture must be purposeful, created by people and for people. It cannot allow for ill-conceived manipulation. It takes into account the influence of factors like the environment, and stakeholders of many kinds, and thus helps people complete a vision by working together. It must be stimulating, inspiring, giving, caring and not judgmental. It must allow people to fully contribute their talents, knowledge and competencies to a vision.

Role of leaders

Culture reflects leadership. Culture can't be expected to become positive and productive itself along the way. Therefore, a visionary must have a vision for culture as well from the very beginning of this long journey.

Being close to people is the leaders' duty and responsibility to maintain a visionary culture. In turn, employees play a critical role in making culture flourish and they need leaders' guidance to ensure it is strong and focused.

No one should forget that whoever controls the culture controls the organisation. Otherwise, if a culture is not managed properly, an organisation becomes unmanageable with little or no chance to complete the vision.

A visionary leader must be professional and able to do a job, expressing care for and understanding of people and share a clear vision of how to get to the future. People will only believe in your vision when they see leaders working on cultivating the same values and meeting the same standards they demand of others. This is about being a model for people.

Mastery of modern leadership can be achieved only by the masterful management of human qualities, cultural values and such essential resources as trust, teamwork, shared vision, accountability, professionalism and innovativeness. A leader who fights for people despite adversity is already winning as people will fight for him and his vision.

Care for people

Under the communist rule of the Soviet Union, an ideology was wrapped around promises of a 'bright future' and all people should sacrifice themselves to the extent of suffering for that promise. This is reflected in a joke – 'to get to communism is a very long journey, and no one promised to provide food and care along the way'.

If the term 'tomorrow' as a noun sounds a bit distant and mystical, care must be grounded in today's needs. A promise of a bright future without care for people today, not tomorrow, is meaningless preaching that leads to a complete loss of people's enthusiasm and engagement. An empty promise like 'all will be fine later' is a sure way to turn the team's effort into a silent resistance. People should feel the benefit from the vision almost immediately.

People will engage only if the company is fully engaged with them. If no care exists in relation to employees, then no engagement can be expected in return.

Care is a verb expressing actions for others, in which involvement with people, concern for their future, emotional comfort, physical comfort and safety are critical elements. The real nature of the company and its vision is seen in its ability to care for people. No team can execute a vision if the culture is fragmented and everyone is pulling in different directions. Only people who combine their energy together can achieve great goals.

Focus and a Strong Will

Execution is successful only if all involved in the vision's creation and execution share the understanding of it and are really willing to make it a reality. They don't point at each other but help each other by pointing in the right direction. They empower each other and help each other, becoming focused into one dynamic force.

I came to Thomas Kolditz asking for his view on what is the core of a vision's execution:

'There's a military saying – when you go to a fight, you fight the fight. You don't fight a plan. The ability to remain agile and work towards a vision is really important. This past week I canceled a major $800,000 project because I lost faith in terms of what it was going to return to us on our investment. Something that had been a part of our broader vision for a long time went away almost overnight. I'm confident that it was the right decision.

One of the principal challenges is to know when a part of the plan or the initiative is no longer important or no longer contributing to what you want because you can't afford to spend resources on things that are not producing and it's not always obvious. When you're an entrepreneur, when you have a vision, you tend to like your vision and don't want to modify it. There's always resistance to a vision that has a lot of ambition to it. You have to determine when the resistance is really warranted and when it's merely the result of small thinking and the inability to really wrap their heads around what you intend to accomplish.

You have to maintain some kind of pressure to keep things moving in a given direction and I think that, in the realm of communication, it has a lot to do with repeating the goals and repeating the vision over and over and it links back to communication again'.

Execution is successful only if all involved have a strong will to see it through. The leaders' role is to maintain the team's will and focus. Think again about Thomas Kolditz's phrase – 'when you go to a fight, you fight the fight. You don't fight a plan'. This is where many businesses fail, being focused on the plans and not the execution of the vision. The prize is a completed vision, not a pile of plans.

To win in this fight, a visionary should help the team to focus on completion and make flexible plans in accordance with a changing reality. No plan can predict and address all challenges that could appear in the course of execution. Life will always throw you curveballs.

Being focused means making rational use of resources for the achievement of this goal. A team with a focused understanding of a goal understands the resources it will require.

Success at any cost is an attitude that sounds desperate rather than effective. It wouldn't attract investors into business, or professionals to join you. No one sensible would be prepared to invest money, time, effort, or reputation into something desperate and ineffective.

Those with a strong will to win become winners, those without a will to win have already lost. Their towel is already thrown in before the first round starts.

A strong will to execute vision inspires the team to fight beyond obstacles. Strong will turns rational decisions into irrational commitment that makes it unstoppable. A strong will makes people stand up after a loss and continue doing what's needed. In other words, nothing great can be achieved without a strong desire and a will to act on it.

Focus is about the clarity of a goal. Mark Thompson is one of the best in the world who knows how clarity of goals is critical for the successful execution of a vision.

Mark Thompson is the world's #1 CEO Coach (Thinkers50 Marshall Goldsmith Awards) and one of the 30 Global Gurus. Mark was the first Fortune 500 CXO (Chief Customer Experience Officer) for Schwab.com, and pioneered MP3 technology as Apple iPod Advisor while Chairman of Rioport. Mark is a Founding Board Member of Esurance.com (sold to Allstate), Interwoven (sold to HP), and Chairman of Integration.com (sold to Silicon Labs). He is a Founding Patron of Richard Branson's Entrepreneurship Centre, Founding Advisor to the Stanford Realtime Venture Design Lab, and Co-Chair & Fellow at the Institute of Coaching Leadership Forum/Harvard-McLean.

Mark is also CEO coach at World Bank, IFC, IMF, Lyft, Pinterest, Qualcomm, Hewlett-Packard, Intel, ADP, Smule, FitBit, FarePortal, Pfizer, IBM, Vodaphone, David Chang's Momofuku and EleVen by Venus Williams.

Forbes listed Mark as a venture investor with the 'Midas' touch. He is a member of the World Business Forum, World Economic Forum and Summit Pioneers. He is a *New York Times* bestselling co-author of *Admired, Now Build a Great Business*, and *Success Built to Last*.

> *'When we think about what the core elements of execution are that would allow saying we nailed the vision, we've delivered on this vision, or how will you know this notion of being able to be crisp and clear about the criteria against which you can measure that vision and hold people and the organization and the systems accountable. This is often missing from one of those big hairy audacious goals and certainly from visions themselves.*
>
> *If you're trying to put a person on the Moon by the end of the decade, well that's on the clock. We know how long it is before the end of the decade. We know that we also want to take at least one person onto the lunar surface.*
>
> *There's another criterion. We know that we want to have quality levels so that we can return them safely. We want to be able to record and capture the experience and bring back the elements of the research that allow us to be better the next time. Those would just be a few criteria that would help us know that once we've achieved the vision, we know that we've delivered on it. Otherwise, it's something that is not very clear to the organization.*

What matters most is what will be delivered in the end. Focus is a central point of attention that pulls the effort of all involved in execution together and defines the deliverables. It must be appealing to all to maintain the will to execute.

If the goals are not clear, people will direct their attention to irrelevant areas, leaving them and leaders frustrated. It is like thinking about driving to Birmingham and asking the navigation system for directions to any city in England and still expecting to reach Birmingham.

Focus defines perspective – what to win, how to win, at what cost to win and when to win. Half the execution battle is won if the focus is set clearly and maintained across the team.

In fact, I have seen many organisations referring to themselves as 'a performing organisation' that mainly are concerned about performing better than last year and not in terms of achievement of a long-term goal. The reason is simple – they don't have clear goals and so nothing to focus on except the past and the present.

You can shift focus if needed and win, but you have nothing to shift if you have no focus. Lack of focus leads to only one scenario – failure.

At the same time, we must consider that execution of a vision takes years. People get tired and a vision gets tired as well. The focus, will and the vision itself need revitalisation. Stuart Crainer has a solution he calls 'shifting focus':

> *'If we think of Jack Welsh, I don't think he had a vision but what he had was a kind of 'shifting focus'. For five years, he said, we're going to be number one or number two in any industry. That was his message and that was the company's basic strategy. He repeated that for five years basically and then it was we're going to make it work out.*
> *I think what I've seen in organizations is a kind of shifting focus because I think even if you have a great vision over time it becomes tired'.*

Execution demands a great deal of persistence and patience. It becomes an energy-draining routine and often takes attention away from a vision. This may lead to a gradual loss of will and engagement. Here we need this shifted focus approach, where execution is split into a number of focused steps, even baby steps, which stimulate revitalisation at certain points. It can be yearly, biannual, or five-year periods where a vision should be revised, revitalised, achievements evaluated – to determine whether execution remains aligned with the vision or demands correction.

Give your team a reason to celebrate their achievements in pursuit of a great goal. This is also a reason to have execution split into stages. Otherwise, tired people easily lose focus.

Communication

Commitment to a vision's completion comes when the team agrees and has a full understanding of it. The role of communication is to align all team members around vision and infuse everyone with clarity, understanding and a sense of engagement. Internal communication secures the transmission of meanings across the company and timely and effective interaction between its members.

Alignment of execution and vision is often lost because of poor internal communication. Strong leaders enhance effective communication and weak leaders convey orders.

We all know how conveying of orders often works. A CEO might say 'I conveyed the order to Mr. Johnston, VP'; Mr. Johnston says that he conveyed the order to Katie Richardson, Head of Department, Katie Richardson claims that she conveyed it to Jim Hill, a manager, and Jim swears that he conveyed it to somebody else, most probably to Alex from two floors below. All meaning and accountability is lost as no one knows Alex and where she works. In any case, she is blamed for everything. In fact, this results in diluting the ownership of execution as no one is responsible and no one clearly understands what to do. Such communication ends up nowhere.

I asked John Spence about core strands of communication that are important for keeping execution aligned with a vision and he shared his time-tested recipe:

> 'There is almost never enough communication of the vision and if people across the organization do not understand the vision it is impossible to align to it and execute it.
>
> And then on execution, there are three main factors. The first one is clarity which is making the vision clear and helping people to understand specifically what success looks like. I call this Extreme Clarity.

Number two is commitment. I need to be absolutely sure that people understand the expectations we have of their performance and what results they are accountable for and that they are 100% committed to delivering them.

It's important to note that commitment to the vision starts at the top of the organization. I'm helping a CEO right now make a major strategic change in his organization and I told him that at some point you've just got to put a stake in the ground and say this is where we're going. It is the leader's passionate commitment to a clear vision that creates certainty in the direction of the organization and allows others to do their best work because they understand what they are trying to accomplish. It is like a strong magnet that draws people together around a common goal.

The last one is coaching – to make sure that people have the support, resources, training and authority necessary to deliver excellent results. Everyone in the organization needs to be aligned with the vision and you've got to constantly keep people focused on it, committed to it and following up to make sure that they understand the role they play in making it happen'.

Three C's mentioned by John Spence – clarity, commitment and coaching, are critical themselves. At the same time, they feed the supreme issue of vision's ownership and whether all team members feel that ownership or not.

If someone feels excluded from communication, or doesn't understand clearly what is going on, or gets disengaged, then he or she has lost a sense of ownership and won't be fighting for progress.

We share ownership by effectively communicating and being magnets for each other. In practice, keeping everyone in sync, particularly in large companies, is challenging and many companies have trouble with this. Yet, if the team's synchronisation is lost, then the execution gets fragmented.

A well-communicated vision pulls all parts of the organisation together towards achievement of the same goal and becomes even more critical in times of change.

Is It Everything?

The aim of this chapter is to emphasise the role of strong leadership and leading people to success.

Execution of a strong and scalable vision is an everyday challenge that must overcome numerous obstacles. This chapter would be endless if we tried to mention all of them.

Still, quality of execution, metrics of a vision, growth and extending a vision and decision-making are essential for helping to align execution with vision and I will discuss them in the chapters that follow.

Practical Tips

- Executing a vision is envisioning success for all and being able to capitalise it for everyone.
- Vision is greater than possible problems and obstacles in execution. Focused execution makes a vision a reality, short-termism kills it.
- If a vision's creation demands imagination, then execution demands nerves of steel and focus on long-term goals.
- People believe in a vision when they see improvement in a leader in the course of execution.
- The easiest way to lose alignment with a vision is when you see something that looks like a great opportunity but is not aligned with your vision. Never take focus away from a vision.
- Culture is a measure of success and a cause of it; it is a desire for success and a way to it; a reality and a secured future at the same time, which demands everyday attention.
- If leaders want their organisations to perform above the ordinary, then they should think culture, speak culture, nurture culture and live culture.

- Leaders invest in people. By adding value to people and helping them to realise their qualities, they are becoming better leaders themselves. Know your potential and help people to explore theirs. This is a perpetual cycle – a good leader makes good employees who make him or her an even better leader.

- People curse things unfamiliar to them or that they don't understand. Communicate your vision and ideas clearly and as many times as needed. A leader who can't or won't communicate his or her ideas will be left alone without followers.

- A shared vision works as an inner code of high engagement and a progressive attitude towards work amongst team members. People consider a shared vision as the main control instrument if they really believe in it. People who feel responsible for achieving vision as their own take collective care of everything that makes control over execution really effective. Control can be achieved through sharing the rights of decisions within the boundaries of that vision.

7

Quality and Metrics of Vision Management

'It is quality rather than quantity that matters'.

Lucius Annaeus Seneca

Many could write a book titled, *Top Thousand Reasons Why It All Went Wrong* and never say a word about the metrics used to gauge progress. Without good metrics and the ability to read them, there is no way to determine how much actual progress is getting made.

Vision management is about being clear what our goals are, and knowing how to meet people's expectations. Without consistent and clear metrics, vision management is just busy work.

Quality

If a vision is a result of quality thinking, then its execution should reflect that quality. A vision only thrives as a result of quality execution. Quality must be a habit from the moment of the vision's creation. A vision succeeds or fails based on the quality of the work put into it.

Amit Kapoor gives central importance to executing a vision:

'Everything is about quality. If I'm not able to deliver that quality, I just lose it, everything just gets lost. You build your vision on quality and you destroy your vision on quality. Even countries can be destroyed by individuals who bet on lousy quality. If you don't pursue vision with quality, it's just actually going to be a lost cause over a period of time'.

Not executing vision with the best possible quality leads to falling into juggling with consequences. We don't talk enough about the quality of execution falling short as the cause of failure in immediate and long-term goals. Crappy work doesn't inspire anyone. Inspiration comes from seeing good quality work on the part of leaders and fellow employees.

We can maintain control over consistency but can't control inconsistency. If allowed, inconsistency takes control over us and everything we do. Therefore, control over the consistency of quality is critical and makes execution simpler and more effective. Consistent and quality work is only possible with full cooperation of the entire team. That requires the leader taking an active and personal interest in the team and the whole process.

The personal touch of a visionary leader can be noticed in every detail of the intelligent direction and skilful execution.

Metrics

Quality of execution and metrics are bound together and reflect the greatness of vision. Yet metrics must be much more than short-term goals celebrated in quarterly reports.

Mark Thompson urges leaders to set metrics as soon as possible to define the direction and set the standards of execution:

'The relationship between quality and the vision is one that's very closely aligned. The first step is I talk about these things in threes to get people to think about how to be able to produce successful results to make it tangible.

The first one is to realize there are many different definitions of quality. The vision should be clear about what quality means. If we're going to put a person on the Moon by the end of the decade, then I think it should be embedded in there that they're going to come home as well.

Initially, getting somebody on the Moon by the end of the decade would be just a big hairy audacious goal. You know what, I'd like to bring him home too.

I think being able to have a shared view of what quality means is another issue. There is a real movement currently, especially among entrepreneurs. I'm based in Silicon Valley. I helped start the Stanford Venture Design Lab. We had something called the Stanford University real-time Venture Design Lab where we were working on trying to identify what are really criteria, what qualities, what traits and what types of vision and people that we needed to create ventures, because it's very risky and most of them fail. How could we improve the likelihood that this great idea will succeed and when we did that, we realized that there was this fundamental shift in the way people were thinking about delivering a product and just getting something out there to the customer the minimum viable product, the MVP.

What's been interesting about that is that it allows you start to curate how the customer or the people who are receiving your services or products would start to embrace your product. They're looking for different kinds of quality.

One of the things that's a common mistake in launching a venture or launching an initiative is we don't have an agreed sense of quality. For some it might mean a beautiful, aesthetically pretty online interface. When I was at Schwab Company, we realized that quality was defined not by appearance but by quickness. In other words, a fast site that loaded quickly that was responsive that allowed the customer to be able to get information really fast.

It didn't have to be all that beautiful, in fact, the more reductionist it was, the more simplified it was the faster it was. Whereas when we started and said, it has to be beautiful but that made it slower it wasn't the kind of quality people wanted.

Understanding this about quality was important to our growth and success. Get clear about that as soon as possible'.

A vision sets expectations and people judge its execution in accordance with those expectations. Metrics should demonstrate to what extent those expectations are met. In the end, the vision will be capitalised based on meeting expectations.

Starbucks began with a vision of providing the best coffee experience. Many people believe they've delivered on that, making the company a global success. Apple delivers on its promises with every new product and increases its capitalisation accordingly. SpaceX surprises people and even shifts expectations further and further and attracts more investors along the way.

Metrics must be challenging enough to encourage people to do their best every day, and clear enough so people know where to focus their efforts. Setting metrics is not about educated guesses, but about being precise as you can't afford even a slight deviation from the goal.

When metrics that should reflect people's desires and expectations are not clearly defined, execution is left to rely on the bottom line and reports full of empty promises. I hardly talk about politicians in this book as the vast majority of them are at a very 'winning' position. Their promises are often very vague allowing people to read into them whatever they want. They deliver no result at the end and only consequences for people to live with. The reason is simple – they don't set metrics, and so the quality of their leadership is a fairly subjective matter.

Visionaries put themselves in a very different position. They assume responsibility for turning expectations into tangible results and capitalise on them. Visionaries understand that metrics must be objective, not subjective. If they are vague, they can be too widely interpreted and become useless.

The metrics of vision must lead to a vision-focused, realistic, appealing, timely and likely result that reflects people's expectations.

Metrics must reflect the core vision's goal. It is critical to understand how long a result will last and if it actually reflects the vision's goal. If the metrics reflect only the bottom line then the vision will not last. You might still have short-term success, but it won't continue into the future. The past year's profit doesn't guarantee sustainable success.

If you set metrics not supported by values people won't commit to the vision. Without metrics that resonate in minds and hearts, people will only feign commitment and enthusiasm.

Timely execution is a sign of a vision's excellence. It can be achieved only if the metrics are clear and timely. Misleading metrics get in the way. They keep execution circling around unimportant goals and tasks that delay the delivery of a vision. When momentum is lost because of the wrong metrics, getting back on track is an enormous and often unachievable task.

Representations of Vision

What would represent your vision? In the end, it's represented not by the bottom line but by quality. This is about constantly asking one simple question – what can be done better? Asking this question and seeking answers to it leads to higher satisfaction and more effective execution. If an idea represents a vision at the beginning, the quality of it represents the vision as it turns into a reality.

Talk to people who are prepared to support your vision and write a full description of their expectations. Based on this, develop metrics which are common and acceptable by all. Your vision will be capitalised on these metrics. Common metrics lead to a commonly ordinary result, while challenging and appealing metrics lead to extraordinary results and extraordinary success.

Practical Tips

- By doing everything with quality you show appreciation to people that believe in your vision. Poor quality is a sign of disrespect to people's expectations and a betrayal of their effort and commitment.

- We always have the possibility to improve quality if we're prepared to admit our shortfalls. If we don't do this voluntarily, then we will be forced to correct them later at a much higher cost.

- Clarity of metrics reflects clarity of solutions to a problem. People invest in your vision if the metrics of it are clear to all, not only for you. Thus, they invest in the meanings that are self-evident and appealing to everyone and give a sense of control and satisfaction.

- In tough times you can give up on many things – scale, processes or deadlines – except quality. At the end of the day, quality is what matters most.

- Vision is an offering of a new level of quality of life and business. Therefore, the quality of its execution should speak for itself.

8

Growth: From Uncertainty to Uncertainty

'Embrace uncertainty. Some of the most beautiful chapters in our lives won't have a title until much later'.

Bob Goff

I must embrace uncertainty to make things certain and then go towards the next uncertainty to grow. The only thing that remains certain is my vision. Uncertainty defines growth while certainty defines stagnation and lack of progress.

People are afraid of uncertainty for no reason. Uncertainty hides the beauty of the unknown that allows us to discover new knowledge and meaning. We define success by making the uncertain certain. Growth lies in uncertainty.

We tend to believe that certainty is a synonym for success because certainty gives a false sense of security. The truth is that certainty is appreciated only by those who are afraid to make a courageous decision to leave their comfort zone. Certainty doesn't demand action, while embracing uncertainty demands real actions that lead to success. We simply ignore the fact that success comes as a result of overcoming challenges and embracing uncertainty.

Where did we get this false belief? Stuart Crainer sees it as a negative heritage from the previous corporate generations.

'In the 1950s and 60s corporations were lulled into a false sense of security that certainty was the reality. In fact, the reality is uncertainty. It is interesting how many leaders are very resilient and very unwilling to accept uncertainty, but they're quite willing to accept it for other people.

They're quite willing to accept that the guy on the lowest wages should have a very uncertain life and very uncertain future but they don't really like it themselves.

The reality is that no corporation has a certain future. They've got to create their own certainties if there are any'.

The myth of certainty and stability is strongly imprinted in many minds. We claim to embrace innovation while resisting it. In today's corporations, people often demand – 'show me something I haven't seen before' and their response to an innovative project is – 'How can I know it will work? No one else had done it before'.

In fact, very few people are prepared to accept uncertainty. One of my Greek clients, let's call him Jason, asked me how to fight uncertainty. My response was – 'Imagine yourself falling through ice on a very frosty winter day. What would you do?' He said – 'I will fight the cold!' – 'You can't fight cold, it is too huge, it is everywhere, it is uncertain and not in your control. You will drain all your energy fighting it and will be dead in a matter of minutes. The only way to survive is to find a solution to get to the shore by ignoring the cold. Uncertainty pushes you to find the best possible solution'.

Jason's reaction was predictable for someone who is afraid of uncertainty. In fact, life is uncertainty itself and the only way to find your way through it is to have a vision that can navigate you through uncertainty.

Uncertainty is always going to be there, and you have to be able to flip it around, get excited about uncertainty, and embrace it. This is part of the process and a visionary must be good at dealing with it.

If you're constantly fighting against uncertainty then you're just getting yourself deeper into trouble while facing more uncertainty. Think of the Buddhist quote that says the minute you stop expecting life to be simple, fair and easy, it becomes simple, fair and easy. Don't waste your energy fighting against uncertainties. Accept uncertainty and make it your way of life. Marcus Aurelius said that the obstacle in the path is the path. Go towards it and do those things that are difficult, and your success is assured.

Vision is a roadmap for change. Mark Thompson sees it as critical for embracing change and leading progress.

'We're at a point in history where the question of mapping a vision is more important than ever before, particularly because we're all facing extraordinary change. There is no organisation, no company, no individual who isn't tormented about change, and having a tangible roadmap for your vision has never been more important. What do we hold constant in the face of change?

We hold a constant vision, a set of values that are driven by our sense of purpose, our sense of impact on the world of the products that we're going to be providing, and our capacity to recruit or bring people together to deliver on that vision.

The transformation that most organisations are going through right now is accepting the uncertainty of change. Change is something that's so challenging for more and more people because there's no one who can escape it. Gandhi said, 'we must live the changes we want to see in the world'. A lot of people will just brace for change out of fear. You have to drive that change or be run over by it'.

Vision is cyclical. It is never achieved but rather constantly refined to go on to the next step. Every time we reach a goal, we go for the next one. It is a path from certainty to uncertainty, then making uncertainty certainty and then embracing uncertainty again.

Phase One: Embracing Uncertainty

Think of a ropewalker. He walks on a rope and doesn't look at what is there far down below while being focused on the goal. He looks beyond uncertainty to certainty. A team faces the same situation as the ropewalker does and should focus on the goal while embracing and working through uncertainty. Here the leader's role in inspiring the team comes forward.

The accomplishment of vision is a team sport. A leader can't move further than his team. The inspired team doesn't need pushing or pulling but only a nudge in the right direction. The ability to inspire is worth a fortune. Teams stand behind every success and no visionary can make it on his or her own. Those who know what big success is know that a strong team is a primary component of this success.

> *Babalola Omoniyi views the team's role as critical – 'If you have the right people and even if you don't have cash, your vision can be accomplished. If you have the wrong people, even if you have all the millions of dollars in the world you will be frustrated'.*

Think of a start-up with a strong vision at the growth stage. An initial team of ten to twenty people is relatively small, and all work enthusiastically hard to make their vision a reality. With time, more people come aboard, and the team grows while more frustration and uncertainty emerge.

Most uncertainty is generated by people themselves. Their doubts, worries and resistance to change feed uncertainty. Those newcomers bring more doubts into the team and the average level of enthusiasm falls. Why? Instead of focusing on recruiting people who share the vision, the focus is only on qualifications, people who eventually create their own silos.

These people don't see anything in it for themselves. This happens with leaders of all ranks as well as shareholders, partners and employees. They are not prepared to leave the comfort zone even under threat of being run over by change. A lot of resistance comes from office silos at all levels. They have a clear under-standing that they wouldn't survive in case of serious change. They are passengers or joyriders.

The silos need to be broken down, and a common language focused on the vision needs to be established. The challenge is to get people to believe in a leader and his vision. People are more likely to believe in a leader and his vision if they see him trying to improve himself, if he also embraces change. To do this, the leader himself has to be committed to the vision and display the enthusiasm that comes with it.

If you don't believe in yourself, then who will believe in you? If you are not enthusiastic about your own endeavours, then who else will be?

Helping people out of their doubts and comfort zones is critical. A leader must be like that confident ropewalker for peo-ple to believe that they can take that chance as well. As Ronald Reagan said, 'the greatest leader is not necessarily the one who does the greatest things. He is the one that gets the people to do the greatest things'.

Asheesh Advani sees the role of a visionary leader as looking beyond uncertainty.

'I think you know embracing uncertainty is challenging for everyone at all times and we are living in a world with more uncertainty, more rapid change and more need for leaders who embrace ambiguity and uncertainty. The great thing about a vision is that it gives you an opportunity to look beyond the uncertainty because you all share something that you're trying to accomplish together'.

How to act in the midst of change and uncertainty? Four principal recommendations come to mind.

1. View the world as a child sees it, as something new and full of opportunity. Every new situation is a chance to learn. Even baby steps will produce results if they are consistent. This will keep you energized and motivated.

2. Your humility is critically important for learning and acting differently. Your experience of a comfortable life can lead you to a false sense of security.

3. Focus on growth, don't focus on uncertainty. If you feed uncertainty, it will only grow. If you nurture and care for your growth, it will happen. Think pragmatically – all these difficulties and challenges that you are facing are opportunities for growth.

4. Communicate your progress and difficulties to show people that you act for them. Consistent communication is a must. Otherwise, people will think that you have left them on their own. It will come to a point where people don't want to be told a story. They would love to be a part of it and they will support the vision when they see its progression.

Phase Two: Arriving at Certainty to Leave It Again

You and your team worked hard to make a vision a reality and reached the stage where that vision benefits many others. Many things that were uncertain are now certain. The vision itself has become certain.

What would happen if Columbus had decided to stay at the Canary Islands and not continue his trip across the Atlantic which was uncertain and challenging? If Columbus had decided to stay at the Canary Islands and not to continue the journey, America would eventually have been discovered anyway but history would be different.

For many, the stage of certainty becomes a place that is difficult to leave. They continue celebrating non-stop and do only one thing – fortify the position of certainty. It becomes a prison without any chance for further growth.

In such cases, comfort and satisfaction can undermine enthusiasm, curiosity and a sense of growth in a big way. Instead of an inner voice shouting 'Bravo', a visionary should hear 'don't get cocky'. This is easily the most dangerous stage. Many nations, companies and individuals get stuck at this stage and don't continue their progression even though they have built an incredible platform for further growth.

This is like Elon Musk's vision for SpaceX after successful launches and recoveries of spacecraft by government agencies had become normal. The doubts and critiques are forgotten, the pain and sleepless nights are left behind. This is a time to celebrate and capitalize on success. SpaceX reached a milestone in 2012 when its *Dragon* spacecraft became the first commercial spacecraft to deliver cargo to and from the International Space Station. Then, in 2017, SpaceX successfully achieved the historic first reflight of an orbital class rocket, and the company now regularly launches flight-proven rockets. Some would have stopped there, but in 2018, SpaceX began launching Falcon Heavy, the world's most powerful operational rocket by a factor of two. On 3 March 2019, *Crew Dragon* docked with the International Space Station becoming the first American spacecraft to autonomously dock with the orbiting laboratory.

If a visionary uses momentum and sees a point of certainty only as a trampoline for the next achievement, the vision grows beyond observable reality. A visionary goes up against uncertainty again and again, growing the vision beyond even its original aspirations.

What is important to celebrate as a team is each other's greatness, celebrate the involvement of supporters and the fact that you can do even more than before. This is a moment when you must clearly articulate that together you become stronger and better and ready for something even more challenging. Take a moment: breathe, regroup and go for the next challenge.

Phase Three: Back to Fight

The red carpet is rolled tightly and put away until the next time certainty is reached. Press releases are filed for the company's history. Congratulatory messages are not interrupting your team anymore. In reality, it takes only a few days for the dust to settle.

Now, it is time to continue the growth. A strong, scalable and compelling vision doesn't grow in a state of certainty. Therefore, constant growth is a universal concern for strong visionaries. They grow by growing their visions beyond uncertainty. This is a moment where men stand strong and boys fail.

Those moments of certainty are the true tests of a vision; can it grow beyond its original scope? Or is it time for an entirely new one? As Mark Twain said, 'the secret of getting ahead is staying ahead'.

Blazing a new trail in the wild means walking in uncertainty for a time. Eventually, you become familiar with the path. The brush is clear, the trees are marked. You know where you want to go and are certain the path will take you there. It's at that point the visionary looks for a new wilderness, fresh uncertainty to conquer. This goes on and on until many paths are certain and followers can use them safely. Many can then benefit from the fruits of the visionary's labours.

We become strong in adverse conditions of uncertainty and become weak resting in a comfortable zone of certainty. Thus, a visionary has an obligation to seek uncertainty as a means of growth. Visionaries seek out uncertainty.

9

Decisions, Decisions, Decisions

'Whenever you see a successful business, someone once made a courageous decision'.

Peter F. Drucker

Vision begins with a firm decision to make a difference. Its success directly depends on the decisive and focused implementation of that decision. Decisions, decisions, decisions. . . they have to be good and often have to be made quickly. The ability to do so separates visionaries from wannabes.

There are no indecisive visionaries. Their decisiveness is refined to the level of an art. A decision to become decisive is the first step to being a successful visionary.

Executing the vision is a chain of decisions. These decisions move you closer to the accomplishment of your goals through many obstacles and challenges. This chain of decisions will either lead to success by being focused on the goal or snapped when decisions become focused on something else.

When executing a vision, a leader must be not an excuse-maker, but a decision-maker – to serve people, to be ethical, to stand firm. This is especially important when dealing with processes that impede the vision. You must decide that you run the process, not the other way around.

Lack of decision-making is often associated with big companies because of multiple hierarchical layers full of people incapable of making decisions or who simply don't care about the vision. Unfortunately, this remains true for all sorts of organisations, not just large ones. The truth is that few leaders are really good at making decisions. They are pretenders rather than decisive leaders.

Arguably, less than 3% of leaders are good at making decisions. This realisation has led me to seek out the roots of this serious issue. Is indecisiveness the result of a lack of vision, organisational environment or something else?

Mark Thompson's superpower is in strong decision-making and he offers a comprehensive view on the problem of indecisiveness:

> 'It's critical to be the driver of your decision-making, to put that vision to use by creating criteria with which you can make easier, more prompt, more direct, and clearer decisions. Only a small fraction of people are great at decision-making and it's because there are three issues that are undermining the capacity to ask and to answer those questions around vision that turn out to create an instant impact on our results.
>
> The first has to be the notion that we may have incentives or disincentives in place in an organization that make it risky to make decisions, that there's more to be protected around the status quo.
>
> The truth is often we don't support the people that we asked to participate in that vision with incentives. In fact, there is a disincentive in that we often don't protect people when they take the risk.
>
> This notion is about being bold in embracing that vision. There are actually systems in place that are undermining the ability of the vast majority of people to make good decisions quickly. The vision ends up being an enabling agent. First of all, by taking away the disincentives and creating an incentive to follow. Secondly, we have to think in terms of clarity. Is there a way to really identify what it means to embrace the vision? Creating some criteria that allow people to act independently at as low a level in the organization as possible is important.

Finally, I think that we don't train people in school to think about multiple choices and we tend to always just provide the right answer. Often in math, we don't take time to derive the equation, we merely have to deliver the answer. I think getting in the habit of providing various scenarios will give people the chance to develop their decision-making capacity. That's part of what I do as a CEO coach. I'm helping people accelerate the capacity for the boss to be able to cascade and train the workforce to make better decisions'.

There are two core properties of decision-making – purpose and enabling, where both are benchmarked against vision and values. Purpose resides in decisions being focused on the vision. Enabling reflects a leader's role in empowering people by providing clarity of purpose, standing for inspiring values, and enhancing decision-making capacity.

Purpose

Vision is the organisation's North Star. It allows people to navigate the challenges the market will inevitably present. Detours may need to be made along the way, but vision keeps you moving in the right direction. Even complex decisions become simple if aligned with a vision and values.

Execution is based on strategy and strategy is based on vision. Vision directly guides decision-making within a straightforward logical chain – compelling vision, comprehensive strategy, focused execution, and clear metrics. This chain is constantly revolving in a closed loop. Every phase of this loop is a chain of decisions which either feed it or snap it beyond recovery. Thus, decisions must be grounded both in the present reality and the future vision.

One of the principal challenges is the ability to say 'no' to promising opportunities outside of the core vision. These are often destructive and take an organisation away from its vision and leave it purposeless.

Thomas Kolditz is a visionary leader who says a firm 'no' to such distracting opportunities.

> *'We benchmark decisions against our vision and mission, and they have to be in perfect alignment with the vision. All of our decision-making revolves around that.*
>
> *For example, we've got a lot of people asking us to do high school leadership processes and programs. But we don't see that as supportive of either our mission or our vision. Our mission is to increase the capacity of Rice's students to lead across the university and then spread that capacity to other universities. That doesn't include being distracted by 10 or 20 million high school students where only maybe 10% of which are leaders anyway. So, we decide not to participate in any of that.*
>
> *We think that the task we have at the university level is enormous. And that's only dealing with a couple of million graduates a year. If we went to the high school level it would be 20 million graduates a year or more. It's just a massive undertaking that no one could get their arms around. Our decision is not to play in that field at all'.*

The quality and focus of decisions reflect the sharpness of the goals. The clearer your goals, the less doubt there should be in making appropriate decisions.

Don't waste time with doubt. This simple formula can save a lot of time and resources. If an opportunity arises that could help your vision but you have doubts about, then reject it. Those who jump on every opportunity don't have the necessary focus on the long-term goals needed to achieve the vision. Maintaining focus long-term is mandatory for those serious about their vision.

Amit Kapoor sees a grand purpose as the most critical evaluator in decision-making:

> *'We know that we want to work in a certain area. This is our purpose so that would determine what it is that we will do and what it is that we will not do. The Institute of Competitiveness actually works in the area of economic geography where we talk about improving the competitiveness of India. When we say "enhancing the competitiveness of*

the country" that clearly means it's about economic development and it's about societal progress. That is what we are really looking at doing and how it fits into the plan. If we are contributing to this vision, we go for it. If not, we reject it'.

There is no success without decisions aligned with a vision. People who can't align their decisions with the values and the vision are stuck in the middle of nowhere. A leader's job is to stick to the values that address vision's purpose and help others see it. Decisions that are misaligned with the vision and its values undermine it.

Values define and guide both hierarchical and peer-to-peer relationships. They determine if an organisation will be a strong whole, heading to a vision, or a bunch of separated units lost in meaningless action.

The aim of values is to stimulate employees and encourage a willingness to commit their capabilities to the achievement of a vision. Values that are accepted and supported by members reach their hearts and minds and allow them to drive an organisation beyond expectations.

No one acts in a vacuum. We necessarily work in collaboration with others. To achieve a strong vision, an organisation must have strong partners. The choice made in employing the right people and choosing the right partners is a principal part of focused decision-making. Strategic development reflects an organisation's real values and shows how it and its employees will act towards customers and partners.

Asheesh Advani addresses hiring the right people as an important part of strategic decision-making:

'Vision influences the kind of people we hire and the kind of people we promote. It influences the kind of partners we work with. It influences the goals we set for ourselves. It influences our financial decisions, human capital decisions, and organisational structure decisions.

I'm in the process right now of hiring some senior executives and one of the ways I'm evaluating the candidates is whether I think they will be good at partnering because our vision is to be an effective partner.

One of the decisions necessary to being a better partner is to have a generous brand. If somebody who doesn't just look out for themselves and is willing to share their assets with others would help us to maximize our impact. A generous brand is willing to let somebody else get fifty one percent of the credit and only take less than half the credit even though you may have done more of the work. I'm trying my best to find people who have been effective partners because I think that is core to our DNA as an organisation'.

Decision-making is the sophisticated operating system that addresses the achievement of a vision at strategic and tactical levels – to what issues attention must be paid and what to ignore, what people to hire, what is urgent and what is important, and what are the next steps to be taken.

To evaluate a decision, it is best to ask whether it is aligned to a vision and pursues its goals or not, and how significantly it helps unlock a solution that brings the organisation closer to its vision.

Discipline in decision-making lays the path to success, undisciplined decisions that chase after every seeming opportunity lead to regret and failure.

Enabling

Decisiveness is a property of a free people. One must be free to be able to make decisions and one must make decisions to remain free. What does it mean? Clear understanding of the goals gives freedom. Freedom is in knowing where to go and what is needed to make this journey.

No one is free if they get caught up in a myriad of conflicting choices and questions that cause more frustration. As a result, such people become hostages of doubt and never move closer to their goals.

Olga Uskova built a global leader in driverless cars by freeing the team in their decisions:

'An ability to make decisions is defined by freedom. You make decisions based on how you see things are supposed to be. This is freedom. If you can't make a decision, then it means that you are not free'.

Garry Ridge is of the same opinion, 'if people are free in a safe environment, amazing things happen'. Freedom enables people's decision-making.

A visionary leader enables and frees people by giving them clear guidance. This is the most productive decision to empower those involved in creating vision and the vision itself. David Katz believes in enhancing independent decisions by involving all in the decision-making process:

'Vision lives inside of every decision. We know exactly where we're going. This allows all people to make independent decisions that are all in the action that leads towards the vision'.

The problem is that most leaders don't allow their people to make decisions. They don't understand that they have a parental role to help others develop their ability to make decisions. A good leader wants thinkers, not spectators.

Such leaders tend to think that their people don't know how to do it, and then wonder why they hired them. These leaders often assume that they would become slaves of those who know answers, but again, why work so hard to hire qualified people if you don't want them to think for themselves?

Leaders often don't communicate the vision effectively to such an extent that people don't know how to make a decision. Leaders need to realise that others can make decisions too. They just need to give their people the freedom to act.

People have difficulty with decision-making because they don't have a grasp of the vision and that means they tend to think of their jobs as meaningless. Without understanding the vision, there is little motivation or ability to make decisions

A clear vision offers a multidimensional framework from which a team can derive their decisions and act. Martin Lindstrom articulated this point very neatly:

> '*I think the vision is a carte blanche cheque you are giving to your future and to your employees. They have a framework they can act within, without having to seek permission every time they make a decision*'.

Trust your employees. If employees have a shared vision, they become an integral part of it and fully committed to it.

Employees' capacity for decision-making is something that should go beyond the job description. If you want your team to be better at decision-making, train them and give them a chance to see their decisions in action. Decision-making is a skill that needs exercising. The more people are trained in decision-making, the more conscious and sharper their decisions become.

If employees are not entrusted with making decisions within their roles, their capacity for decision-making suffers. As a result, a leader who doesn't entrust people to make decisions only encourages silos, not professionals.

An organisation's capacity for decision-making begins with a leader's capacity to make a final decision. If a leader is indecisive or hasn't had sufficient freedom to make such decisions, this causes stagnation across the whole organisation.

Sania Ansari sees the importance of sufficient capacity for decision-making for those who are in charge of the final decisions:

> '*You cannot give a decision to someone incapable. If someone was entrusted to run a company with over fifty million dollars turnover and expectations of what he should do with it are set, where this person does not share the same vision and has only two million dollar company experience, then this person wouldn't be able to make appropriate decisions and drive the company to success. He should work hard to grow a capacity for decision-making at a higher level and how to stay aligned with the vision*'.

An incapable leader can kill a business, leaving it a pile of rubble. This happens far too often. Execution doesn't tolerate procrastination or incapacity to make a decision or indifference. Such leaders are more concerned about protecting their status quo and there is no point in expecting them to support people with their initiatives and decisions.

A visionary leader and no one else sets the direction for all team members by embracing a vision and putting in place a system of enabling and empowering people to contribute with their decisions. A visionary is a model from whom people learn to maximise their capacities in decision-making.

Purpose and Enabled Capacity

When we think about decision-making, we usually think of getting the right answers. However, what seems like the right answer now can be detrimental to the vision in the long run. Therefore, the visionaries' duty is to clearly define the purpose and help their teams to think long-term.

On 26 September 1983, the firm decision of Stanislav Petrov, Lt. Colonel of the Soviet Air Defence Forces saved the planet from a nuclear disaster. On that day, the Soviet Union missile attack early warning system 'Oko' displayed a 'LAUNCH' signal in large red letters accompanied by a lot of blaring alarms. The screens showed that five American intercontinental ballistic missiles had been launched against the Soviet Union.

Stanislav Petrov didn't report the incoming strike as he judged it to be a false alarm, while clearly realising that he was acting against military protocol. Later, the investigation revealed that a newly established early-warning system mistook the sun's reflection off clouds for missiles.

In those days, the Soviet Union had 1.5 times more nuclear missiles than the USA. If Petrov had pushed the button, then the most devastating catastrophe in human history would have wiped out millions of lives in a matter of minutes. According to the

Congress's Office of Technology Assessment report (1979) such an attack and the subsequent mutual strikes would have killed between 136 and 288 million.

The decision of one person taking his responsibility seriously prevented a large-scale nuclear war and saved the planet. Stanislav Petrov was thinking about the consequences of his decision in terms of immediate impact, indirect impact, and postponed effect, and probably saved all our lives.

Practical Tips

- Focus on the vision and determine how every decision is connected to the vision.
- A leader shouldn't be surprised by growing office silos and lack of initiative and creativity if he or she lacks decision-making capacity. This is a result of his or her weak leadership.
- The more a leader coaches employees in decision-making and bold thinking, the more powerful an organisation becomes, and the more time for development this leader has.
- Set people free by allowing them to make their own decisions. Leaders who try to stay safe by not making decisions make others hostages, resulting in stagnation and death of a vision.
- No one said that decisions are easy, particularly at the strategic level, but it is still a skill that must be trained to the highest possible level. This skill is essential if you think about being a visionary leader.

10

Vision as a Business Tool

'I dream of painting and then I paint my dream'.

Vincent Van Gogh

Brilliant ideas are valuable but the ability to apply them in a simple way is key. How to turn vision into a practical tool? This is a power question raised by all people I know in relation to personal and business life. I've been asked this question by many at all levels of professional life. 'Have you ever thought about the roles and functions of shamans?' Yes, you read it right, about the North American or Siberian shamans. My friend, Rose Cameron, an exceptional mind in cultural anthropology, brand strategy and innovations suggested – 'while you are exploring vision, why not to look at shamans who act as mediators between the normal world and the world of spirits. Look at them as visionaries or those who connect people with something beyond the obvious'.

In all relevant cultures, a shaman is considered as someone who 'sees', a chief person of knowledge, the intellectual and spiritual leader in their community. One of their important traits is that they have to free themselves from ego and give full attention to help people face the future with confidence. Helping leaders become visionaries is like helping them become the shamans of the future.

Let's look at vision as a business tool by bringing everything discussed so far together.

Vision as a Business Tool

Success is the result of thoughtful, well-structured and future-looking actions. Yet, the vast majority of organisations tend to use their previous achievements and previous financial statements as predictors of future success. In fact, historical data is not reliable in terms of predicting the future and have limited value in determining where the organisation is going.

Forward thinking triggers changes because you're pushing forward in new areas. You're leading and helping your people. You're moving in a direction that other people didn't know was possible. A visionary is not just coming up with a dream or a vision but backs it up with data, research and feedback constantly, paying attention to how they relate to the vision.

Vision is the foundation for success at any stage of an organisation's lifecycle. It is the most reliable tool for leading people to the prospective future. However, it is not automatic. It demands discipline of the mind and structured actions towards achievement of the goal.

Vision execution is a continuous process of activities, inputs and outcomes. Every stage demands feedback loops and evaluation of progress. This allows the organisation to remain agile, improving and strengthening all processes, controlling its development, make appropriate decisions and putting ideas into action.

Vision as a business tool consists of six stages – creation, visionary growth, construction, communication, execution and continued growth and change. Yet, we must consider that every phase involves internal and external discovery. Every phase must be purposeful, motivational and keep everything aligned to the vision.

Figure 10.1 CAVIAR process.

Vision is a process that can be defined by a simple term, CAVIAR, as it stands on six pillars – clarity, ability, viability, influence, acting and revitalising.

See vision as a business tool diagram in Figure 10.1.

Clarity from a Moment of Creation

Vision bridges today's reality with the future reality by creating the future in advance. It does this by working towards future solutions to present needs. Vision is a statement that reflects an organisation's reason to exist. It begins with a conscious awareness of a problem that needs to be solved.

It is your decision to make a difference for the world. Your irresistible aspiration to solve a grand problem for the benefit of others will attract others.

Vision comes only when your conscious awareness of a problem and craving to solve it reaches its peak. Ask two simple questions when thinking about a reason for your vision to exist – What would make the world different from your vision being implemented? What is the value for people in your vision? Your vision will become a super magnet for people if you have meaningful answers to both questions and it is worth turning it into a reality. If you can't answer these two questions meaningfully, then this is just a project or idea that demands deep refining. Clarity of a vision creation stage presented in Figure 10.2.

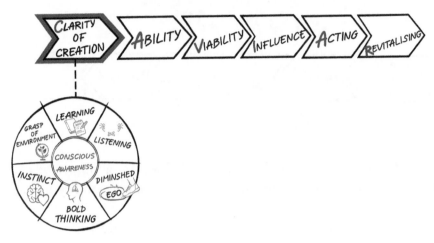

Figure 10.2 Clarity of creation stage.

A vision elevates a visionary giving him or her a better view of the future and aspiration gives strength to make it a reality. This comes with conscious awareness. Conscious awareness of a problem is not enough, regardless of how strong it is. It must be supported by learning, listening, diminished ego to a state of selfishness, broad outlook, a full grasp of environment, bold thinking and enhanced instincts that resonate with the world. These elements define how much one knows about the problem and the difference to be made.

Vision comes to those who consciously educate themselves and scrupulously work on elaborating their understanding of the problem they aim to solve. It takes its time and doesn't come overnight. Think of the years it took for a strong and compelling vision get created and defined for the likes of Marshall Goldsmith, David Katz, John Spence and other visionaries. No one creates something exceptional without knowing enough about it and how to create it.

In simple terms, vision comes when a visionary has clarity on what problem he or she aims to solve. Clarity of the grand goal and how to make it a reality defines the strength of a vision.

This organically feeds the next stage of a vision creation – a visionary self-development and growth or a visionary team self-growth.

Ability to Make It a Reality

A leader's capability to turn vision into a reality directly depends on well-developed visionary leadership traits and competencies. Self-awareness, emotional intelligence, learning, courageous thinking, self-discipline, all come into play because no one can manage something as huge as a vision without being sufficiently prepared.

Facing unchartered territories and being prepared to lead people to a desired destination demands consistent growth. A visionary leader must constantly improve and develop his capabilities.

No one can lead a change without changing themselves. Being a visionary leader demands a great deal of time, learning, communicating and constantly looking for ways to move forward and grow.

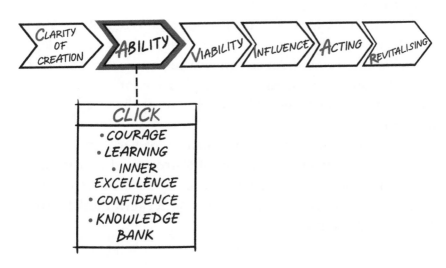

Figure 10.3 Ability.

I offered a well-tested and efficient CLICK self-assessment form in Chapter 3, Fighting Anti-Visionary Me, which helps to develop the core properties of visionary leadership – courage, learning, inner excellence, confidence and credibility and knowledge. I recommend returning to it often as a way to evaluate your development. Ability stage is presented in Figure 10.2.

Courageous thinking is essential for the creation of a strong and vivid vision. Every long and difficult journey begins with a courageous decision. Vision demands courage as does any exploration. Courage is mandatory for those striving to create and execute a great vision.

Learning is critical for meeting every new challenge. Learning means growth and transformation. Learning allows us to understand our goals and how to get there. Without learning, we can't become who we want to be.

No one is perfect, but getting better and growing in excellence is a leader's responsibility. This requires life-long mental training. Leaders build their own selves so they can better serve others, as a leader's growth is limited by psychological and emotional unpreparedness. A drive to achieve inner excellence is critical.

Confidence, in a way, means defeating yourself over and over. It means defeating your fears and anxieties, your tendency to procrastinate. Confidence comes when one is sure that he or she fulfils and even surpasses his or her commitments to customers and employees. The leader must be credible and authentic.

No leader can move further than his or her team's competencies allow. Therefore, creation of a strong and ever-growing knowledge bank is essential where every team member must contribute to growth and nourish his or her own thinking from this jointly created source.

Viability of a Vision

Vision defines why and where effort should be placed. Leadership is blind without a clear and robust vision. Thus, a vision must be clear so that leaders know how best to direct their team.

The construction of a vision must be purposeful, manageable, flexible and dynamic. When the construction is clear, we can spot faults in our efforts and correct them as needed.

Everyone seeks viability and reliability in a vision whether you are an investor seeking to invest into something rewarding, a professional looking for the best application of his or her competencies as a potential employee, or a customer looking for the best product.

A vision's viability can be checked against the six criteria of vision – stimulus, scale, scanning, spotlight, simplicity and excitement and passion.

Every criterion depends on quality and measurability. Vision is strong if quality is maintained from the beginning to the end product. How quality is measured should be determined at the beginning and flow naturally from the vision.

Measuring or evaluating a vision before committing to it should be the norm. Clear construction allows a vision and the progress in fulfilling it to be gauged, allowing you to make changes along the way. Viability of vision or six criteria of a strong vision presented in Figure 10.4.

Stimulus. Vision must clearly demonstrate a commitment to serve people and solve their problems. Without stimulus, the vision collapses immediately because it is not grounded in people and their desires. For instance, both David Katz's and Feyzi Fatehi's visions are perfect in their purpose to serve people and offer solutions to significant problems.

Scale. A vision is strong and compelling if it allows you to explore new opportunities as it grows. A vision dies if it does not

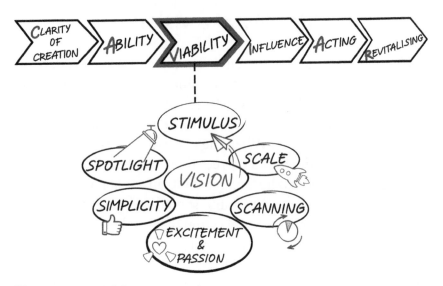

Figure 10.4 Viability.

grow. Scale is directly linked to the response to stimulus as can be seen in the growth of the WD-40 Company. People in 176 countries consider WD-40 spray as a must-have product and the demand continues to grow strong.

Spotlight. Vision presumes an obligation to immediate stakeholders as well as future generations. The visionary is responsible for the impact, both negative and positive of his or her vision. Vision without responsibility is just personal ambition at a cost to others, or gambling with the resources of others. The visionary must also explore opportunities that are directly related to stimulus and scale.

Scanning. Vision demands a keen eye for where and how value can be added and how to do so. The blind vision disappears unnoticed. Do you feel the slightest wind of change that could grow into a market storm? Keep scanning every day to spot new opportunities and stay relevant.

Simplicity. The sophistication of vision is in its simplicity. Vision assumes finding the simplest solutions and answers to the most complex problems. A complicated vision is groundless and not connected with people and thus does not easily overcome challenges. David Katz's vision wouldn't be as appealing, executable and growing if it were complicated.

Excitement and Passion. There is no engagement without passion and vision is not an exception. Vision should create positive emotions in others who in turn add value to the vision. The power of hearts united by an emotionally rich stimulus in response to unspoken desires makes a vision really compelling. A vision that doesn't address passion is not scalable. If people are not attracted to the vision, it won't grow.

The sustainability of a vision is in its ability to withstand many challenges. If one of the criteria doesn't withstand a test, the whole vision is shown not to be viable as the whole construct will collapse when it finally faces a strong challenge.

Influence

Vision strives to engage people and expand its influence through effective communication. The issue is, how do you get people to be part of a story and actively share it? Influence is visualised in Figure 10.5.

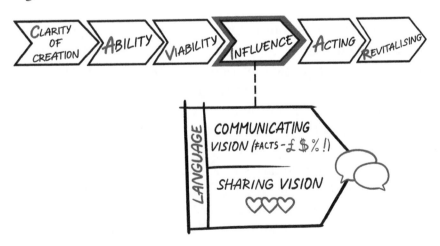

Figure 10.5 Influence.

We already discussed that the ability to multiply that gift strongly depends on the leader's ability to influence. The greater the vision, the greater the need for strong and far-reaching influence. The success of vision greatly depends on the effectiveness of consistent communication in challenging times and the celebration of achieving milestones.

Vision is a constant dialogue and exchange of energy and not a one-man show where people are just listeners without any chance for interaction. People will tune out if they are not able to contribute.

Social capital is critical for the building of a base of believers and supporters. This support is necessary to creating a robust network based on mutual commitment and understanding.

Minds and hearts tend to open to warm, authentic, insightful and intelligent messages that are delivered in a manner relevant to everyone. The message to be communicated must be clear, purposeful and effective, expanding influence even in challenging times.

In fact, many organisations suffer because of ineffective communication. They have difficulty communicating a vision even inside their board room and hardly talk with their people. Thus, their calls for action sound more like a scream.

How effective is your communication? Does it open minds and hearts and trigger appropriate actions? The vision should cause a positive response in people. If it doesn't, it appears to be disconnected from people and its processes are fragmented and not executable. There is little if any chance to pull all the pieces of vision together without clear, consistent and effective communication.

All successful visionaries put a great deal of time and effort into communicating and sharing their visions and engage others and influence more and more people by doing so. How much effort do you put into communicating and sharing vision? How do you communicate gratitude to your team for their effort and achievements?

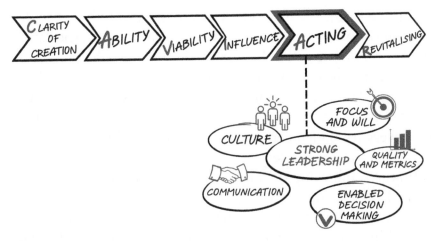

Figure 10.6 Acting.

Acting

Vision shows its importance and beauty in its execution where visionary leadership requires action and results. Those hiding behind intentions continue avoiding the future, in capable of making it a reality.

The vision reveals its appeal and beauty if executed artfully by a strong, visionary leader. The greater the vision, the stronger the leadership it demands. That strong leadership allows maintaining the focus and will to complete a vision and demands cultivation of a strong culture, enabling decision making, effective internal communication, high quality and clear metrics. See Figure 10.6.

Culture

Culture reflects a common goal that people aim to achieve together wrapped in a shared vision. A visionary doesn't lead a vision. He or she leads people to success defined by the vision. Thus, strong leadership depends on a circle of well-developed competencies in encouraging growth and leading people to success. This demands mastery in cultivating culture and being a model for people, as with Garry Ridge in the continuing success of WD-40 Company or David Katz's mastery in uniting people and inspiring them for the exponential growth of the Plastic Bank.

Vision as interaction between the future and the present is rooted in the productive interaction between people, which is only possible if culture is productive. Culture is the energy that drives a company to success. Every positive input and energy from every team member is needed to achieve a big goal.

What culture do you cultivate in your business – positive and future-embracing or fragmented and stale? Do you stimulate and enhance that necessary energy or only talk about it? The answers will show what your team could achieve under your leadership – success for all, or political games where all stand blaming others for failure. Never forget that culture reflects leadership.

Focus and will

A clear, vivid and well-communicated vision and strategy for growth, driven forward by a culture of disciplined execution and accountability has no place for illusions or empty promises. It strives to infuse the team with focus and will, getting everyone to pull in one direction and together to become an incredible force in achieving a goal.

If you, as a visionary leader, have promised people they will achieve something great you have to help them stay focused on it. In their turn, people will be focused on a vision and exercising a strong will to make it a reality if they see these qualities in their leaders. Neither Doerr Institute for New Leaders led by Thomas Kolditz or Institute of One World Leadership led by Noel Ferguson would be successful without focus on their goals and the entire teams' will to make a positive and lasting difference.

Where is your focus? If your focus is on the bottom line, the team's focus will be there as well undermining execution of the vision.

Communication

Communication affects the connectedness of all involved executing a vision – employees, partners and customers. If it isn't efficient, clear and proactive your stakeholders will feel isolated and so fail to contribute.

Many learn the hard way that the solution lies in productive partnerships as no company can thrive on its own. A company can create incredibly promising strategy that will never leave the planning stage without effective communication to all involved.

Think of how Marshall Goldsmith communicates his vision and goals with his team, partners and followers. Marshall communicates value to all, encouraging more engagement with every communication. The quality of Marshall's communication reflects the quality and value of his vision for everyone involved.

Gaps in communication demonstrate either a team's or a partner's ineffectiveness and must be addressed immediately. If you ignore those gaps, you might deprive yourself of valuable feedback exactly when it is needed. No battle can be won by disconnected units and no vision can be completed by people who don't hear each other.

Quality and metrics

Without clear and vision-centred metrics, the whole journey is a pure gamble. It is impossible to reach a destination without knowing what it is. Metrics show the destination, and quality standards show the desired level of mastery needed to execute the goal. Therefore, metrics must be set clearly and accepted by all involved.

If execution gives up on quality, then metrics can't be met. If metrics are doubtful, then quality will suffer. If execution shifts focus away from the desired metrics, then no report can hide it. This is a signal that your team has lost its direction and must be realigned with the vision.

How clearly does your company's reporting system demonstrate the necessary metrics and consistency of quality standards? Check as often as possible because every detour may lead to failure.

Enabled decision-making

Enabled decision-making helps to navigate uncertainty to the desired destination. When people are free knowing where to go and what they aim to achieve, they generate incredibly valuable ideas and make well-balanced decisions. They realise that their decision must generate solutions and value, not more problems, and direct their thoughts and actions accordingly.

People empowered to make decisions become giants who make execution possible regardless of the project's complexity. They maintain control over the execution like it's their own child. They grow and make the vision more compelling by adding more value to it.

Do you enable decision-making and encourage your team to contribute or do you lead in an old-fashioned dictatorship style? The latter leads to fear of mistakes, which in turn restricts effective execution.

Revitalising by Embracing Growth and Change

Vision dies if it doesn't grow. Successful completion of a vision leads to a self-amplifying chain of events. A strong and scalable vision goes from execution to thinking about the next goal and so on. A true vision starts a chain of events that allows it to grow beyond what was originally envisioned.

At the same time, a compelling vision assumes sustainability, that assumes continuity of growth and positive impact at every stage of development. In this sense, the sustainability of vision reflects its connectedness with reality.

Figure 10.7   Revitalising.

Vision grows like a snowball until the impact is on a global scale, positively affecting millions. It consists of several action steps in a cycle. As the vision grows, its energy must grow from stage to stage, and from achievement to achievement. See Figure 10.7.

Intel's founders radically changed direction in 1985. Intel Corporation was the largest manufacturer of memory chips in the world when, in 1985, its founders, Andy Grove and Gordon Moore realised that the demand for their memory chips was going down as Japanese competitors came with memory chips at below-cost price. They were forced to make radical change. They realised that given the pattern of how fast memory was improving, and how much cheaper it would be in 10 years, they would not be able to make any money. They foresaw that Intel must get out of the memory business because it would die otherwise. They decided to do microprocessors and they're now the number one microprocessor facility in the world.

Andy Grove had the vision and Gordon Moore had the technological know-how for them to make that shift. They had the massive courage and vision to step from certainty to uncertainty and won.

From a personal standpoint, when people have experienced extraordinary achievement, they crave to discover more about themselves and their inner potential. This is a natural need for people to release their energy creating something positive. The horizon beckons irresistibly those who know in which direction to grow.

A number of indicators can be used to evaluate continuity of growth – market response and demand, continuous expansion and growing influence, changes in technology and many more.

Even a simple indicator, like elaborated creativity, can be used for evaluating consistency of growth. Consistent growth demands consistent creativity in finding new solutions and approaches to achieving a goal in the most efficient way. When a vision becomes stale, it doesn't demand or encourage creativity. You become stuck in certainty and the comfort that comes with it becomes like a weight keeping you down.

Every strong vision should be like a good book or movie; it should keep you wanting more.

Keeping Tension

Businesses far too often only seek to grow the bottom line. They create fake and catchy vision statements to attract investors while focusing on quantity and ignoring quality. These companies cannot handle inevitable market changes and die when the first storm hits.

Successful vision is determined by the structured and focused approach to its creation and execution. Structure and clarity always beat a non-systematic approach however genius it is. The CAVIAR approach allows you to evaluate where you are at any stage of your vision's journey and keep the tension between where you are and where you want to be.

The need to modify the vision and end-state is especially true, as organisations need agility balanced with thoughtful decision-making that allow them to grow. This business tool allows vision to be modified where needed, keeping it versatile and practical.

Part IV

Visionary You

11

Fifteen Commandments of Visionaries

'Success is not final, failure is not fatal: it is the courage to continue that counts'.

Winston Churchill

A re you interested to know how visionaries think? I've always been interested to learn what makes them so unique and successful. For me, understanding their habits of thinking and acting is like having a key to the seventh wonder of the world. What does it mean to be in a room with visionaries? It is incredibly interesting and inspiring to understand these genius minds who change the world every day.

While talking about vision, how to create and execute it, I believe it is crucial to open a window into how visionaries think and act. These strong leaders determine much of the future we will live in. They do this by providing a compelling vision of the future. They achieve not by being merely aspirational but by combining those aspirations with a pragmatic, goal-oriented lifestyle.

Long ago I noticed that visionaries are very good at recognising each other. They flock together like birds of a feather. This begs the question – how do they recognise each other?

What are the traits they all share? And what makes people feel so inspired and uplifted after talking with them?

Every article about visionary leaders talks about their traits. We all know that they are hardworking, creative, accountable, confident, very self-disciplined and excellent communicators. They are very good at saying 'no' and are exceptional decision-makers. Visionaries' values are always aligned with their purpose. These traits are fairly obvious.

The most interesting traits remain hidden behind the scenes. Underneath the surface are certain traits shared by all visionaries. These are what differentiate a good and talented leader from a visionary.

There are fifteen commandments or strong traits that make visionaries strong and successful leaders for the future.

1. In personal or business life, we mainly hear people talk about their problems, often without even being interested in solutions. Whether they be family members, friends or colleagues, they want you to be dragged into their swamp of problems without even moving a finger. Finding solutions to their own problems is even not on the agenda for many.

    Visionaries are very different creatures. They talk solutions, not problems. They thrive by finding solutions. This is their passion. Visionaries are well aware of problems everyone else talks about. They just don't waste time talking about them except in the context of trying to find solutions. They are attuned to finding opportunities to turn a situation from negative to positive. It's no wonder that Winston Churchill said, 'The optimist sees opportunity in every danger, the pessimist sees danger in every opportunity'.

2. We often demand support from friends and family for a new endeavour or to help us in a difficult time. Often, when we ask for support, it causes resistance and criticism rather than encouragement and support. Instead of pushing each other up to a higher purpose, people tend to drag each other down

to their level. Envy leads people to prevent others from succeeding. Visionaries push others up, helping others realise their highest purpose. They grow by helping others grow. The lesson I've learned over the years and effectively use in my consulting and coaching practice is that we are all here to reveal the greatness of each other.

3. Visionaries see their role as creating more and more value every moment, every day. Value added is what defines their level of success. Money is secondary, coming as a result of acting and adding value to everything they do. Actually, they rarely talk about money. Their desire to find solutions is greater than their egos.

4. Visionaries have an incredible ability to make an impact in a short amount of time. They are able to open new horizons in just a few phrases. I remember my first conversations with every visionary I ever met as if it were yesterday. They have a charisma that reaches you in your core and inspires you to action.

5. The visionary is at peace with change. Rather than resisting it, the visionary seeks out and implements the change that will help people the most. What some see as a destructive storm, the visionary sees as something that gives life, watering seeds that will bear fruit in due time.

   A visionary is not someone scared of a storm, but the storm himself or herself that causes even more storms. These storms bring value through the change they bring.

6. Envisioning the future demands purity of mind. Visionaries use the mind for its primary purpose, for deep thinking and developing ideas. They keep their mind free from irrelevant information rather than polluting it with nonsense. One of the simplest and most effective ways of doing this is limiting their use of modern gadgets. Don't get me wrong, they are all very good at using these clever things. But they are not chained to them. I never see any one of

them staring meaninglessly at the screen or playing with the phone just to kill time.

7. Can you see a difference in following – being ready to fail and being prepared to start again after a failure? Visionaries are not just prepared to fail. They are willing to start again. They are patient and persistent, willing to deploy their own resources and sacrifice themselves for their goals.

8. They know how to win against themselves, against the odds and against any competitors. They breed winners and celebrate their success. Wining for the sake of the future means breaking boundaries of common opinion and ignoring stereotypes. Visionaries make fun of those boundaries.

9. Visionaries consciously and unconsciously use a flow formula – humility, plus learning, plus curiosity, plus courage, plus discipline. Humility allows them to admit that there is always something to learn. Willingness and ability to learn makes them realise they are 'a work in progress' and become better every day. Curiosity sparks their craving for exploring something new. Courage is needed to go beyond themselves and manage something huge and yet unknown. Discipline is critical to making things happen.

10. They love what they do and their love is not troubled because of difficulties. This is a real love that feeds passion and optimism. Passion and optimism help to have a strong hope for success and pursue it until the very end.

    Once you grasp it, you become addicted to such passion and optimism and the way they affect life and business.

11. Visionaries manage energy, not time. For visionaries, time is not a critical reference point. Rather, energy utilised and value created is more important. No one can leave time as a legacy but the achievement brought about through a visionary's use of energy can be a legacy for generations.

12. They have a keen eye for seeing the uniqueness in ordinary things and finding inspiration in everything around them. This allows them to explore the world for themselves and others from very different angles. Their broad outlook allows them to connect often unrelated things.

13. Visionaries are big on simplicity and clarity. They are simple in speech, in life habits, in enjoying life, in interacting with people, about themselves. Simplicity raised to the level of art defines their exceptionally structured thinking. They don't beat around the bush but get straight to the point by asking precise questions that lead to the answers needed and offer very well-structured explanations. Structured thinking allows visionaries to create sophisticated and effective algorithms for building huge and complex things in a very simple manner.

14. Visionaries develop their inner senses to the highest possible level. Their instinct is a very powerful and versatile tool, almost a scientifically precise one. This quality feeds their ability to spot opportunities and groundbreaking ideas even before it can be rationally explained. Thus, their inner voice serves them as the best and wisest servant.

15. A majority of people consider themselves as systems that are bound by certain inputs, dependencies, contexts and predefined capacities. This keeps people from seeing an abundance of opportunities. Visionaries make themselves open systems that interact with the environment and universe. They open themselves to a higher purpose. They accept uncertainty and unpredictability. At a certain point in life they said to themselves – 'Yes, I'm very small but I am a part of something huge, eternal and I'm an important part of it'.

Don't Call them Futurists

A visionary and a futurist are very different creatures. A futurist will tell you that climate change will lead to the end of civilisation and there will be tons of refugees and refugees will create war. That's what a futurist will tell you.

A visionary will tell you – the young people of the world should have the skills and motivation to be able to solve any problem, including climate change. They want to help young people solve the problem of climate change by educating them. As a result, we will not have refugees and not have problems with professional education, which is aspirational and pragmatic.

Futurists draw a dreary or even scary picture of the future where visionaries create a positive future. A visionary is someone with a tangible plan as he sees where he is going and where to lead people. A visionary creates the future and will sacrifice themselves for it.

Olga Uskova commented on the difference between futurists and visionaries from a very practical standpoint,

> *'For the last five years, none of the futurists' predictions came true. Futurists working for audiences and for a short period of time sell what people want to hear. Any forecasts or crystal ball predictions, particularly those I see regarding the driverless vehicles, are fakes in reality'.*

There are a lot of things like health care artificial intelligence, synthetic music computers, deep learning, augmented reality and many more innovations that futurists don't predict. Visionaries define the implications of those new inventions and spread them globally. Visionaries materialise the present and use a path to the future that exists in the here and now. In this sense, I love how John Spence defines himself – 'I'm a todayist'.

Be the Same

Be fair, we all make empty promises – I will go to the gym next Monday, I will definitely read about such and such topic next month, I will start learning about this or that thing soon, and so on. No one will believe in our empty promises for long, not even us. As a result, the vision disappears like a morning fog.

What makes visionaries different? They are disciplined in fulfilling promises to themselves and to others. They focus on a vision, not themselves. These traits are not necessarily extraordinary. They have the potential to exist in all of us.

You can do this. There is only a great gain in adapting these traits. See what you already have in terms of being well developed and what needs improvement and keep building up. All is in your hands. Let's start today.

12

I Believe That. . .

I believe that we can change the world and the way we live and work by the power of positive and bold thinking. Our thoughts are alive, and nothing is more beautiful than a bold fresh idea that is brought into the world.

Since I can remember I've been very curious about two things. My 'why' was related to what restricts my dreams and 'how' I can do things differently to make life more interesting. I was thinking beyond what would be expected from a boy whose late childhood was in Monchegorsk at Kola Peninsula, one of those small towns founded around Stalin's gulags in the cold Arctic territories of northern Russia. In such places people are condemned to live a dull life of drudgery with little hope of improvement. Most of my classmates didn't make it to their fiftieth birthday.

Life put me through different experiences – from facing gale eleven storms on a small trawler in the middle of the Atlantic Ocean to the successful execution of global-scale business projects highlighted in the international media, from having nothing at hand to being considered among the elite of global thought leaders.

A few years back I found myself in a tough professional crisis after some heavy losses. I was exhausted, losing self-confidence and had no clear idea of where to go. My previous achievements actually held me back, restricting forward-thinking and keeping me in a cycle, making the same mental mistakes again and again.

One day I asked myself a simple question – What is greater, my goals and dreams or my problems? My goals, without a doubt! The answer was so obvious and powerful that it hit me like a bolt of lightning.

I realised that if I was aiming to reach goals beyond my immediate needs, beyond my comfort zone, I needed to explore and adopt new ways of thinking every time I aimed for something new. I must find newer and deeper meaning at every stage of my life and professional development.

Life is meaningless and empty unless I make it meaningful. I'm responsible for making my life meaningful. The greatest beauty in the world is a fulfilled life. I steal from the world if I'm not using my life purposefully.

As soon as I shifted my focus from myself to the world, I saw the beauties of this world, the awesomeness of tranquillity, the miracle of a storm. I learned that I expand myself by giving and adding value to others and helping them grow.

When we travel across continents, we know we need to recover from the jet lag. When we begin to develop a vision, we mentally travel in time, from the present into the future and need to consider mind lag, the difference between the present state of mind and one that is sufficient for the future we envision. Having vision means closing this mind gap towards the future.

Our thoughts have the power to make a positive impact on the way we live and work. We are the masters of our evolution and are not merely the results of mindless processes. Positive visionary thinking defines a man-made evolution as a parallel to natural evolution. How positive our future is depends greatly on how we envision it and how we are willing to work to make that vision a reality.

I believe that vision grows through being fed by knowledge, experience, instincts, bold and positive thinking; and when conscious awareness about what I want to do reaches its peak, I can whisper into the future's ears what I want and it will agree and offer the answers.

Changing the world for the better is difficult. Many have tried and failed. It demands dedication, vision and hard work. But it starts with a thought. When that thought becomes a fully developed vision, solutions to inevitable problems will present themselves.

Responsible Decision

Vision is a decision to live differently, with greater purpose. This is a very personal and conscious decision, not a random choice. This is a conscious choice made in the full knowledge that the path is difficult and success will be the result of long and hard work.

One of my clients once said to me – 'Vision is great, of course. But how to choose between two great visionaries and their visions?' My answer was simple – 'Create your own vision if you want to change something for good using your own desires and capacity'. Everyone is responsible for their own decision to reach the summit of their lives.

Do not allow anyone to silence your vision. Vision gives that crucial forward view for those brave enough to look into the eyes of the future and take a chance. Don't hold on to your anchor when you have sails and wind.

Heritage

Vision comes with responsibility for future generations. This is our duty, mine and yours, to empower others as soon as we decide to take the role of visionary leaders. Strong vision never dies. We are responsible for the legacy we leave and for being a model for future generations. The next generation must be greater visionaries and we must give them that important spark. We are a living example for the next generation and what we do now and the way we think has a direct impact on how the next generation will go further.

This is particularly critical now when incredible changes are forthcoming. We can foresee a new generation that will redefine capitalism in a more conscious, ethical way, where positive societal impact is as important as profits. As the world is becoming more connected, people are realizing that we have tremendous social and environmental problems that must be dealt with and social responsibility becomes a true global movement, rather than just a paragraph on a shareholder annual report. We take responsibility for developing trust between generations. Our generation gains the trust of the next generation based on real facts and achievements. Our results are artefacts for future generations.

I'm still on a search for the golden ratio of vision. Even so, this journey has been valuable as it has allowed me to find answers to many critical questions and to explore vision as a practical business tool. This opens incredible opportunities for many ventures across the globe that will make a positive impact on the future of millions.

I am deeply touched and sincerely grateful that you have taken part in that journey, exploring vision and making it a practical tool for others.

I hope that this discussion has helped you gain a greater understanding of vision as the fundamental force behind every great success, to question the status quo and boldly present new perspectives on old ideologies.

You are stronger than you think and have already become much better as a leader. Now it is your turn to become a co-creator of a positive future by adding the power of your own vision. Your vision defines your own life and business success and the success of others. Start creating your success today, right now.

Acknowledgements

Vision is an eternal and never-ending creation that changes the lives of others. This is a journey that demands the contribution of those who know where to go. I'm deeply grateful to the visionaries who contributed to the creation of this book. Marshall Goldsmith, Martin Lindstrom, Garry Ridge, David Katz, Stuart Crainer, John Spence, Feyzi Fatehi, Olga Uskova, Asheesh Advani, Adam Witty, Sania A. Ansari, Thomas Kolditz, Alex Goryachev, Noel Ferguson, Amit Kapoor, Nabhit Kapur, Raphael Louis and Babalola Omoniyi – your support, comments and shared wisdom are greatly appreciated.

This journey cannot be completed without the support of those who believe in me. I thank my wife, Zagidat, for the incredible support and for sharing the pressure during this journey.

I take my hat off in praise of the support and very special contributions from two of my dear friends – Carmel de Nahlik and Rose Cameron. I'm blessed by your help.

Carmel de Nahlik always has insightful comments and bold ideas that help me to add more perspectives to the discussion. I wish everyone had such a friend who always helps to grow and explore new dimensions and fields.

The mind-expanding discussions with Rose Cameron – about who we are, what we do as visionary leaders, what we see around us and what we can change – infused me with inspiration and energy to dig deeper into the phenomenon of vision and to see something incredible in ordinary things.

I am very grateful for the exceptional effort from Eric Postma for his invaluable editorial suggestions, comments and overall support.

References

Darabont, F. (1994). *The Shawshank Redemption*. Hollywood: Columbia Pictures.

Einstein, A. (1929). Einstein interview in *The Saturday Evening Post*. Online https://quoteinvestigator.com/2013/01/01/einstein-imagination/ (accessed 21 July 2019).

Foote, M. and Douglas, C. (1997). *Visions: Notes of the Seminar Given in 1930–1934 by C.G. Jung*. Princeton, NJ: Princeton University Press, pp. 131–132.

Gaiman, N. and Pratchett, T. (2011). *Good Omens*. London: Transworld Digital; Media tie-in edition.

Meisner, G.B. (2018). *The Golden Ratio: The Divine Beauty of Mathematics*. New York: Race Point Publishing, p. 60.

Pattakos, A., Dundon, E., and Covey, S. (2017). *Prisoners of Our Thoughts: Viktor Frankl's Principles for Discovering Meaning in Life and Work*. San Francisco: Berrett-Koehler Publishers, p. ix.

Viscott, D. (1993). *Finding Your Strength in Difficult Times: A Book of Meditations*. Chicago: Contemporary Books, p. 12.

Index